MAXIMIZING BASEBALL PRACTICE

John Winkin, EdD
with
Jay Kemble, MA
Michael Coutts, MA

University of Maine

Human Kinetics

Library of Congress Cataloging-in-Publication Data

Winkin, John
    Maximizing baseball practice / John Winkin, Jay Kemble, Michael
Coutts.
      p.   cm.
    Includes index.
    ISBN 0-87322-430-2
    1. Baseball--Training. I. Kemble, Jay, 1963- . II. Coutts,
Michael, 1959- . III. Title.
GV875.6.W56   1995
796.357'07--dc20

                                                            94-14633
                                                                CIP

ISBN: 0-87322-430-2

Human Kinetics books are available at special discounts for bulk purchase. Special editions or book excerpts can also be created to specification. For details, contact the Special Sales Manager at Human Kinetics.

Developmental Editor: Mary E. Fowler; **Assistant Editors:** Ed Giles, Kirby Mittelmeier, Henry Woolsey, Karen Bojda; **Copyeditor:** John Wentworth; **Proofreader:** Kathy Bennett; **Indexer:** Barbara Cohen; **Book Designer:** Stuart Cartwright; **Typesetters:** Stuart Cartwright, Ruby Zimmerman; **Illustrators:** Alex Moore, Stuart Cartwright; **Photographers:** Monte Rand, Damon Kieson; **Cover Design:** Keith Blomberg; **Cover Photographer:** Will Zehr; **Printer:** United Graphics

Printed in the United States of America   10 9 8 7 6 5

Human Kinetics
Web site: http://www.humankinetics.com/

United States: Human Kinetics, P.O. Box 5076, Champaign, IL 61825-5076
1-800-747-4457
e-mail: humank@hkusa.com

Canada: Human Kinetics, 475 Devonshire Road, Unit 100, Windsor, ON N8Y 2L5
1-800-465-7301 (in Canada only)
e-mail: humank@hkcanada.com

Europe: Human Kinetics, P.O. Box IW14, Leeds LS16 6TR, United Kingdom
+44 (0)113-278 1708
e-mail: humank@hkeurope.com

Australia: Human Kinetics, 57A Price Avenue, Lower Mitcham, South Australia 5062
(08) 82771555
e-mail: humank@hkaustralia.com

New Zealand: Human Kinetics, P.O. Box 105-231, Auckland Central
09-523-3462
e-mail: humank@hknewz.com

To all the players who have worn a Maine uniform, for making the program what it is today and to those who have carried their love for the game into professional baseball and coaching.

Contents

Foreword

Baseball, without question, is the greatest game of all. Athletes of all ages, heights, and builds can play it. And natural ability and favorable working conditions can take a player only so far. In baseball, a deficit in talent and the absence of an ideal practice facility can be overcome by superior effort and smarts. Success comes to those who work hard to make the most of what they have.

John Winkin has been proving this for many years with his University of Maine baseball program. Season after season, John and his players overcome their wintery climate and limited indoor practice conditions and are one of the top teams in NCAA Division I baseball. And because Maine players are taught and drilled so well in baseball fundamentals, you can bet that two or three of John's players will be selected each year when Major League Baseball holds its draft.

Now, in *Maximizing Baseball Practice*, Coach Winkin shares his secrets for effective practice instruction and game preparation. No matter where or what level you coach, you and your team can benefit from the information in this book. Even you veteran coaches who have had success and believe that your practices are as good as they can be will find worthwhile suggestions to make your practice sessions better.

Tommy Lasorda
Former Manager, Los Angeles Dodgers

Preface

Better practice makes better play. So it's not surprising that the best and most consistent baseball teams and players make every minute of practice count. *Maximizing Baseball Practice* is a synthesis of what we have learned through the thousands of practice sessions that have led to our more than 900 wins. Success doesn't just happen—*you* make it happen. And there's no better place to start than in practice.

Whatever level you coach and in whatever location or climate, the way you conduct practice will be shown in your team's performance. *Maximizing Baseball Practice* will help you develop practice sessions that maximize the performance of your team. We'll describe to you the ideas and drills that have made our program successful, and then we'll show you how to implement them in your own practice sessions.

Although indoor practice sessions are not ideal, for many teams they are necessary. To be successful at the University of Maine, we've had to make the most of our many indoor workouts. We've streamlined the organization of our practice so that the entire session runs like clockwork. No matter what your climate, *Maximizing Baseball Practice* will help you develop more efficient and productive practice sessions to better prepare your team for next season (or next game).

During practice, how well you prepare your team depends on your ability to organize time, use space efficiently, teach the mastery of basic, fundamental baseball skills, and simulate game situations. Your practice priorities will reflect your coaching philosophy. Practice efficiency—getting the most out of each minute—is a priority for all coaches. Our top five priorities in developing great practices are:

1. developing the endurance of pitchers with an emphasis on proper pitching mechanics,
2. mastering the basic skills,
3. mastering defensive skills,
4. developing hitters, and
5. developing knowledge of game situations and reacting properly to any batted ball, attempted bunt, attempted steal, and emerging rundown situation.

These priorities determine how we set our practice plan and use our time and facilities. If your number-1 priority is hitting, you will organize your practice session around hitting. Whatever your priority, use all of your time and space, involve as many players as possible, and plan your priorities to best develop your team for game situations.

In presenting our information, we assume that all athletes involved in your practices are in top physical condition. We begin the book by sharing our methods for getting the most out of your players' use of their time and facility. You will learn how to organize your practice to take advantage of every bit of space. You will learn which drills best suit your circumstances. You will learn to prioritize your roster so that those most likely to play get the needed repetitions for the coming season. And you will learn to treat every practice like a game.

In Part II we break down the practice session, indicating how to benefit most from drills and other activities within your practice space and time. We prioritize 28 drills for pitchers, catchers, infielders, and outfielders and show you how to fit the drills into your practice sessions.

Part III covers the fundamentals: fielding, hitting, and baserunning. But because players must be able to perform these skills in game situations—in cooperation with team objectives—we also address the important step of bringing the individuals together to develop team unity. Along the way, we'll introduce you to team philosophies, position drills, and team drills.

We are not "gimmick" coaches. We do not believe in fancy pick-off plays or in developing players who can make the occasional flashy play but have trouble making the basic play consistently. Consistency wins ball games. We believe in practicing the basic skills, whether pitching, catching, fielding, throwing, or hitting, until the skill becomes automatic and can be performed consistently, day in, day out.

We also believe in player safety—an important issue when practicing indoors. Throughout the book we stress the importance of player protection from caroming balls through the use of netting and proper protective equipment. Please note that photos accompanying descriptions of the drills are for illustrative purposes only. Catchers and hitters should always wear protective equipment during practice drills.

Setting and implementing priorities and developing practice sessions is not easy. You need to commit yourself to developing a successful program. If you take the time to analyze and adjust your practices to suit your needs and circumstances, you are well on your way to winning.

Maximizing Baseball Practice provides the blueprint for developing practice sessions to meet the needs and goals of your team. Whether you are getting ready for the first day of practice or preparing for the playoffs, we hope you find the time to read, learn, and enjoy. The time spent reading this book can save you countless wasted hours of inefficient, unproductive practice sessions. And it just might help you and your team to achieve the best reward in baseball—a championship season.

PART I
Practice Planning

We all know the feeling of having a team with so many weaknesses that we don't know where to start. Setting priorities can be challenging. The importance of planning ideas, goals, and objectives can weigh on your mind every day.

Before the preseason begins, our coaching staff meets and discusses our available players and how we can best develop them for the coming season. We try always to answer these questions:

Who will pitch?
Who will catch?
Who will hit, and in what order?
Who will be our position players?
What is our strategy in relation to team defense?
How can we develop our players through live experiences?

These questions are a good starting place and can give you a perspective on your philosophy and what lies ahead. In developing your philosophy and setting priorities, consider how much time and space you have in which to practice. One of your top practice priorities is determining how best to teach your players what they need to know to handle game situations.

At the University of Maine, we spend 7 to 8 weeks indoors preparing our team to compete with many of the top-ranked college programs in the country. We must share our facility with the varsity softball team, and the men's and women's track-and-field squads. Consequently, when we are able to use the facility, we must make the most of the opportunity.

In Part I you'll see how we develop our daily practice sessions to take advantage of the time and space available. We'll show you how we make full use of our facility and involve as many players as possible in each segment of our practice sessions. We'll present valuable tips on planning and implementing the most efficient ways to conduct your drills. And, finally, we'll share how we organize and schedule practice, making the best use of equipment and player personnel.

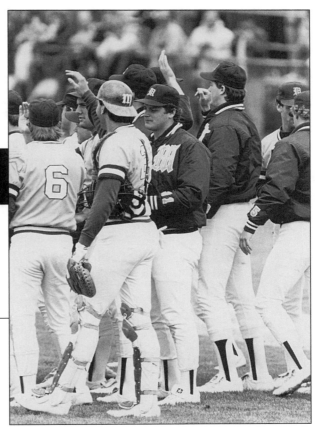

CHAPTER 1
Maximizing Time

Time is one of our most valued commodities. Once it is gone, there is no way to get it back. Time wasted is a loss to everyone involved.

As a coaching staff we spend 60 to 180 minutes a day developing our daily practice session. The best way to prepare our baseball team is to spend the necessary time developing practice so that when our players arrive they know exactly what to do when. By planning ahead, we know that every minute will be filled with a drill or routine that will help develop our team.

The National Collegiate Athletic Association (NCAA) has restrictions on the amount of time college teams can practice each week and on how many days each week a player can practice. Many of you face similar restrictions, especially high school coaches, who are allowed just 3 weeks of preseason practice and no Sunday sessions. Because of these restrictions you must continually evaluate your use of time.

IDENTIFYING YOUR PRIORITIES

There never seems to be enough time to be as good as you want to be. But if you plan well, you will reduce the potential for wasting time (and you can use any time left at the end of practice to repeat individual skill work or practice specific game-situation drills). Prioritize your available time to fit the needs in developing your team. A quick, organized practice that involves every player is the most effective way to do this. Always keep your players active. Having players stand around is not only boring for them, it can be a disadvantage for the entire team.

The first step in prioritizing is to analyze your time. How much practice time do you have each day? Our practices run between 2 and 2-1/2 hours a day; any time beyond that is usually nonproductive.

Your next step is to identify your goal for the day and what you must do to accomplish it. As we said in the Preface, our top priority at Maine is to develop the endurance of our pitchers. Pitchers take the longest to get ready, are the most vulnerable to injury, and require the most attention, so we organize our practices around building their endurance. This is what we plan to spend the most time on in every practice.

In the preseason we require our pitchers to throw a specified number of pitches each day. As the season draws closer, we increase the number of pitches required. Regardless of the number of pitches, we have the same goal every day: to build the endurance of the pitchers so they can comfortably make their pitch counts each outing. This usually involves about 1 hour of practice. Meanwhile, the infielders, outfielders, and hitters are involved in drillwork. During live hitting, basic skills are scheduled for the everyday players.

Once we know our time limits and are preparing practice schedules, we can begin to work on our pitching needs. We then fit the practice for the other players—fielding drills, team defense, baserunning, and so forth—into their remaining slots, as described in the next section.

ALLOCATING YOUR TIME

Fortunately, our facilities allow us to practice pitching and hitting at the same time by having live pitching throw to live hitting. Although pitchers require a great amount of time each day, it is critical for you to allot enough time to develop the rest of your team as well.

We allot about 15 minutes a day for each individual position player to perform drills to develop the basic skills of his position (these drills are outlined in Part II). We spend 15 minutes each with infielders, outfielders, catchers, and pitchers on developing individual skills such as fielding, throwing, footwork, and handwork. This takes about 1 hour of practice. Once these individual skills are completed, we allot 15 to 30 minutes for team defense, such as developing knowledge of game situations and reacting properly to any batted ball, attempted bunt, attempted steal, and emerging rundown situation.

We are fortunate to have a practice facility large enough to allow all our players to get their necessary repetitions. Dividing our facilities into two sections allows us to focus, plan practice, and develop situations where our players master the necessary skills within the time available. When time is allotted for use in the basic skills area, we concentrate on building the team as a unit. We focus on individual skill work for a set period of time and then bring the players together to develop them into a team. This ensures that all of our projected starting players will learn to work together and, likewise, with the reserve players. Once time has expired in the basic skills area, we move to pitching and hitting.

DIVIDING YOUR PRACTICE

If 2 hours have been allotted for practice and you allocate 1 hour to practicing basic skills, try using the following example in scheduling your practice.

In the first hour of practice focus on basic skills as planned. Organize each area of basic skills within a time frame. Each time frame should run for 10 to 15 minutes as emphasis is placed on pitcher drills, infield ball handling, outfield drills, catcher drills, and team defense. Devote the second hour to endurance pitching and hitting in the designated pitching and hitting area. (*Note*—daily practice schedules are discussed in chapter 4.)

The focus of the second 60 minutes is to develop skills through game situations. Pitchers and hitters will battle one another in the hitting area while the everyday players continue to work on infield ball handling, outfield, and catcher drills.

If you do not have a specific hitting and pitching area available, all drills will have to be done within the 2-hour period. While one group is hitting and pitching, another group should work on basic fielding skills. The players will continually rotate until all players have completed their repetitions. Additional strategies for scheduling practices based on certain space considerations are detailed in the next chapter.

CHAPTER 2
Maximizing Space

Time is not the only factor in developing effective practice sessions. Space is just as important, especially for teams that must practice indoors. Well-developed practices make full use of all available space and involve as many players as possible. When planning practices, evaluate the space available and use it to your advantage.

If you are a team that practices indoors—whether it be inside a large fieldhouse or a small gymnasium—you can still well prepare your team for the coming season if you organize your practice carefully. In developing safe and appropriate indoor practice facilities, focus on three important factors: facility size, division of the facility, and protective equipment. These factors should play an important role in your thinking as you develop the most efficient and effective practice plan.

DEFINING AVAILABLE SPACE

As much as you would like to practice in a domed stadium, reality and practicality tells us it is just not going to happen. So you must develop practices that can fit within the framework of your facility without causing you to compromise your philosophy.

Gyms and practice facilities come in all shapes and sizes. Most high schools have a facility the size of a gymnasium basketball court. When more funds are available, as with colleges and universities, the larger and better equipped the practice facility can be. The larger the facility, the easier it is to prioritize practice and develop realistic, game situations involving the most players at one time. In smaller facilities, the need to prioritize is greater. If you have a basketball court–size facility, for instance, you may be able to do only one or two drills at once, so fewer players will get the ideal number of repetitions. In such a case, your most critical priority in preparing your team should receive the most attention.

The better you use space, the more involved each player can be. And the more repetitions a player gets, the better he gets. Our goal as coaches is to involve every player for every minute of practice. At Maine, we can create game situations involving a complete infield with live pitching and hitting. Many programs, unfortunately, do not have that luxury and must adjust accordingly. That doesn't mean that these programs cannot be successful. For example, many teams that must practice indoors don't have the opportunity to practice on a regular size infield until their very first game. If this is your team's situation, you can still be successful by using your facility to enable your players to practice drill after drill and develop sound fundamental skills. It takes only a day or two to adjust to the outside.

As coaches, we often don't realize how much space we actually have. Do you really use all available space? For instance, do you use part of your gymnasium's stage to do a hitting drill? Do you use the hallway for baserunning? Do you use a classroom to teach basic skills and a chalkboard to teach situations? Many coaches are surprised at the amount of space really available to them once they choose to be creative and resourceful.

DIVIDING YOUR SPACE

As we discussed in the previous chapter, it is important to divide your time into two areas: hitting and pitching, and basic skills. Divide your space in the same way. Have your pitching and hitting area available at a moment's notice so you can develop practices that focus on live pitching and hitting without taking time away from basic skills drills. Also, you won't have to rush building your pitchers' endurance, and you can spend as much time as you need on pitchers and hitters.

Using two different areas also allows your players enough space to complete the necessary repetitions for proper development. While one group of players—say, the infielders and pitchers—work in the live hitting and pitching area, the outfielders can work in the basic skills area (see Figure 2.1). Once the first group has completed their repetitions, another group of pitchers and the outfielders can get their repetitions in the hitting and pitching area while the infielders get theirs in the basic skills area.

The Pitching and Hitting Area

A separate area for pitching and hitting allows you the flexibility of concentrating on developing an effective batting order while you also build the endurance of the pitchers. This area also allows you to move the pitchers and hitters into different near-game experiences by working the top pitchers against the top hitters. Again, if possible, the pitching and hitting area should be available to you at any time and should include an area for pitchers to warm up. This area may be one edge of the gymnasium, a vacant classroom, or an unused stage. Regardless of its location, the area needs to be well lighted, netted, and at least 70 feet long and 10 feet wide. Two hitting cages would be ideal.

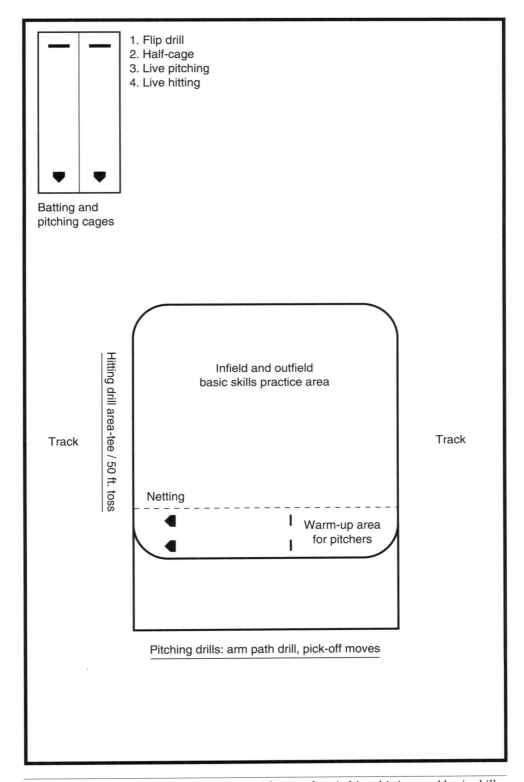

1. Flip drill
2. Half-cage
3. Live pitching
4. Live hitting

Batting and
pitching cages

Track

Hitting drill area-tee / 50 ft. toss

Infield and outfield
basic skills practice area

Netting

Warm-up area
for pitchers

Track

Pitching drills: arm path drill, pick-off moves

Figure 2.1   Sample indoor practice set-up with areas for pitching, hitting, and basic skills.

The Basic Skills Area

The basic skills area is a large facility with ample room for your players to master pitchers' fielding, infield ball handling, outfield communication, catching, and team defense (see Figure 2.2). Likely, this area will be a gymnasium or common area to which each in-season athletic team has time allocated each day. The larger the area, the easier it is to make the drills game-like and to place your fielders at real distance when working on individual and team drills.

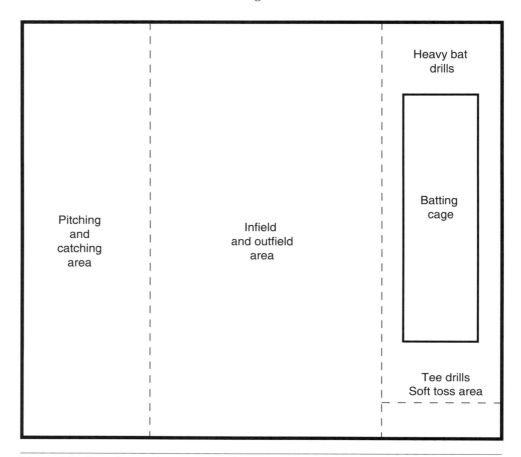

Figure 2.2   Sample practice set-up in a large gymnasium with 1 batting cage.

For safety, the basic skills area should be well lighted and, if possible, completely netted to keep balls from getting away and hitting nonparticipants. All glassed areas should be covered or screened and walls padded for player protection.

Dividing Space in a Single Area

Most high school facilities are small and do not allow for two separate practice areas. If this is your situation, you need to analyze the space available and develop a way for your team to take advantage of it. Prioritize your space to fit your needs. Figures 2.3 through 2.6 show ways to divide available space based on different needs and facility sizes. Most coaches in this situation will have only one major area to work in. This area is commonly a large gymnasium with a batting cage extending from one end to the other.

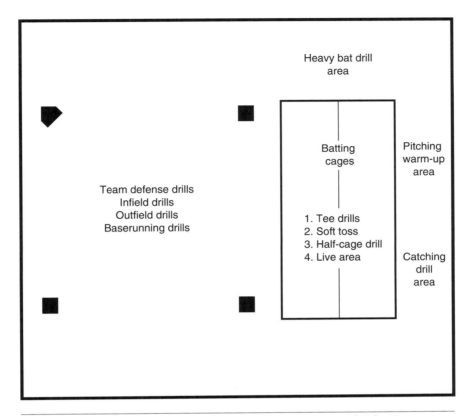

Figure 2.3 Sample set-up in a medium-sized gymnasium with 2 batting cages.

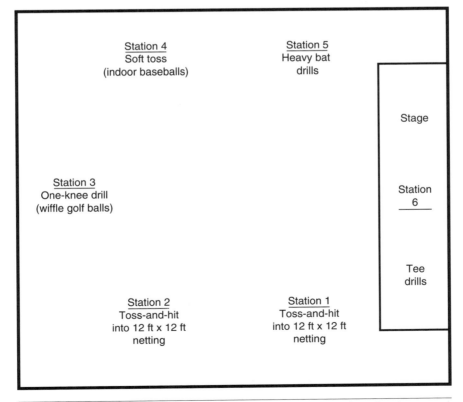

Figure 2.4 Sample practice set-up in a small gymnasium with no batting cage.

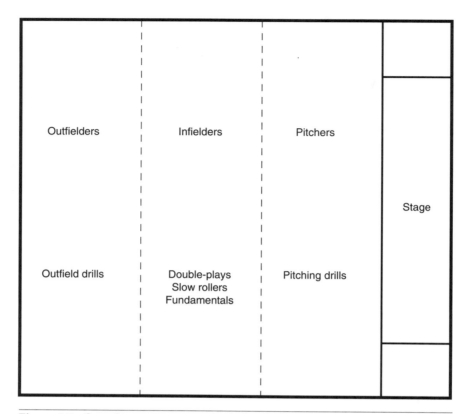

Figure 2.5 Sample practice set-up for individual team defense drills in a small gymnasium with no batting cage.

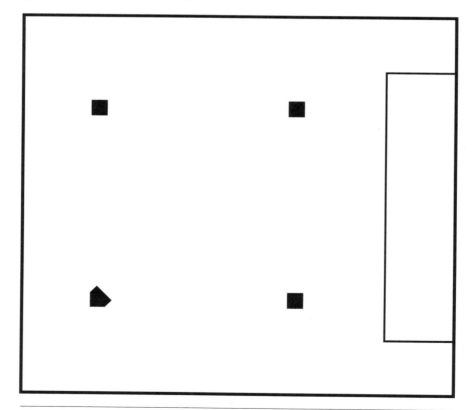

Figure 2.6 Sample practice set-up for team defense drills in a small gymnasium with no batting cage.

If you coach in a program with limited practice space, try spending 3 days a week, such as Monday, Wednesday, and Friday, developing pitchers and hitters. Designate one area for only hitting and pitching and develop stations to keep the players involved in these two activities. You can designate Tuesday, Thursday, and Saturday for basic skills and team defense. On those days, incorporate drills to develop the necessary skills planned for that day.

Again, develop a system that allows your top players and top pitchers to get the quality repetitions they need to prepare for the coming season.

Coach's Corner

My two current assistant coaches both coached at the high school level and practiced in facilities whose space limitations allowed for only one practice area. They made full use of what was available, organized their practices efficiently, got the most out of their practices, and they both were very successful. That's why I hired them.

PROTECTIVE PRACTICE EQUIPMENT

No matter how small or large your practice facility may be, it is not complete without protective equipment. The more protection you have for your players, the less they have to worry about injury and the more they can concentrate on developing basic skills.

The chances of your players sustaining injury are magnified when practicing indoors. The equipment you have available should influence how you develop practice. Here is a list of equipment necessary to make indoor practice safe and enjoyable:

> Proper lighting
> Safety netting
> Area nets
> Pull mats
> Batting cages
> L-screens and square screens
> Portable mounds

We'll discuss each of these items briefly in the sections that follow.

Proper Lighting

Organized practices usually involve many drills taking place at once. The number of people and the dangers of using bats and balls make good lighting essential for safety. If players have to squint to see what is going on, either they need glasses or your facility is too dark. Remember that all lighting, as well as all clocks, windows, and any other objects that will easily break, must be covered to protect them from being hit by balls.

Safety Netting

Safety netting is important for the protection of your players and nonpartici-pants. Enclosing the complete practice area with netting is ideal, but this can be very expensive. The more enclosed the area, the less chance there is for injury and subsequent liability. Any batting area must be entirely enclosed for safety. The more areas you have netted, padded, or protected, the more productive your practices will be.

Area Nets

Area nets give you flexibility in developing practice. Use them to separate the batting cage so that twice as many players can hit at the same time. Area nets allow you to separate groups and involve more drills.

Pull Mats

Pull mats should be placed on walls that remain uncovered by netting. Uncovered walls pose a danger. A baseball that hits an exposed wall ricochets quickly. Players tend to follow a ball. If a ball is poorly thrown and passes a player, the player tends to turn to get it. A ball ricocheting off a wall can carom back and injure an unsuspecting player.

Batting Cages

A caged batting area enables you to use the rest of the facility for basic skills. When possible, a batting cage should be 90 feet long, 10 feet wide, well lighted, and entirely enclosed. This area is essential in developing a team because it will be used for live pitching and hitting, or hitting against a pitching machine.

L-Screens and Square Screens

L-screens and square screens are used for both indoor and outdoor practices to protect players and coaches from stray balls. For example, place an L-screen in front of the pitcher's mound to protect the pitcher from being hit by a line-drive hit directly back at him. L-screens are especially important indoors, as there isn't a lot of room for the pitcher to move and the glares of the walls often hide hit balls.

Place square screens in front of bases to protect the fielders. For example, with a square screen placed in front of second base, the middle infielders can practice double-plays while another group practices another drill. Any ball thrown wildly will hit the screen instead of the middle infielders.

Portable Mounds

Indoors, pitchers should throw off of portable mounds. Such mounds are 10 inches high. Each portable mound should have a pitching rubber and a front, sloping decline that resembles a real mound. They are useful in the live pitching and hitting area or for pitchers to warm up on. Their portability helps allow you flexibility in developing practices.

CHAPTER 3
Conducting Practice

Everyone knows that organization is the foundation of success. Success in baseball is no different. Developing a good baseball team is a season-long project, and organization is crucial.

PLANNING AND IMPLEMENTING PRACTICE

Plan efficient practice sessions in which all players know their responsibilities at all times. If a player knows he is to be involved in fielding drills at 3:25, he should be ready to begin at 3:25. If he is not responsible enough to be ready on time, he should lose his position on the team to someone who is. Don't allow wasted time.

Coach's Corner

I had a player who graduated from Maine a few years back. He was a great talent but never lived up to his potential because he was not responsible enough to handle his duties at practice. He was often slow or late getting to a drill; he didn't always hustle, and sometimes he gave a half-hearted effort. I evaluated his desire and confronted him about his effort. He said he would work harder. He never did, and he was beaten out by a lesser talent.

Players who know their roles and duties better understand the goals of each practice. This understanding promotes harmony and allows players to focus on developing the fundamental skills needed to win games. How well a player recognizes his duties also gives you a starting point for judging his desire. Practice can become monotonous, but players who work the hardest to get better will prove themselves in drills. The best talent does not always turn in the best performance.

Players should not only be responsible for playing and practicing—they should be responsible for helping in all aspects of the program. As you develop practices, ask players to set up and move equipment when necessary. Ask players not involved for a set of drills to help run other drills. Ask older players, who have been involved with the program longer, to coach and lead the younger players who may not have yet grasped a particular system. Some of our players at Maine have been great leaders in helping the younger players develop. They have been through the routine and often have an easier time of explaining a drill than we do.

Staffing Practice

Few will dispute that baseball is a complex game with many different facets. Hitting, pitching, catching, defense, and offense are just a few of the aspects of the game. With the limited number of head coaches involved, assistants who understand the game and who are loyal to the program are critical.

As a head coach, you cannot be in all places at once. Often, due to limited time and space, many different drills will have to be run simultaneously for practice to be efficient. Use your assistants wisely to benefit the program. Give them responsibilities, and then hold them accountable for their work. If they are loyal to you, their decisions will be based on the best interests of the program.

Team Unity

For success, all physical aspects of the team must be finely tuned and ready for play. The same can be said for the team's mental aspects. Dissension causes confusion. If some members cannot focus on the game, the chance of all players giving their best effort is decreased. To develop team unity and loyalty, you must integrate as many team functions within practice as possible. This includes, but is not limited to, stretching, conditioning, team meetings, and drills.

We like to begin practice with a quick team meeting to explain the plan for the day and to describe any new drills or ideas we are trying. This meeting usually lasts about 2 minutes. We also stretch and cool down as a team, and we end each practice with another team meeting. Any player with something to say about that day's practice or anything else is able to speak at that point.

Coordinating Drills

Effective practices require well-organized, efficiently run drills. Each player should be instructed and drilled at his individual position. Once the player has learned the proper techniques of his position, he must be taught the finer aspects of the game. Then, and only then, are you ready to bring the team together as a whole.

All practices should be conducted in the same manner. Each player should practice individual skills such as ball handling or pitching mechanics. Once this has been completed, the player is ready to begin position work. We like our players to drill position work with partners. This allows them to coach and push each other to become better. Once each player has finished his position work, all players are brought together for team work.

ORGANIZING YOUR PLAYERS

Understanding player personnel is critical. Organizing player personnel may be the most difficult aspect of developing practice. To best organize your players, you need to determine who will be given priority on quality experiences during limited practice time and space. Patience and careful analysis of the available talent is needed to make last-minute decisions and changes in practice schedules. This is an area of coaching that needs to be adjusted just prior to practice, most often due to class schedule conflicts, illness, or other unexpected circumstances.

You can plan for some of these situations in advance. Check class schedules or the absentee list to know who will and will not be at practice. We require an ill player to inform us by 10:00 that morning so we can make adjustments. Our team rule is that he must see a doctor to get clearance before he can practice again.

Evaluating Your Players

As you begin practice in early spring, develop your schedules and prioritize personnel on the assumption that you know what your players can and cannot do. For many high school coaches the problem of insufficient time to prepare is magnified because state rules dictate the time during which teams may practice and prepare. Most high school preseason baseball programs are limited to 3 to 4 weeks in the spring and no time at all in the fall. This of course does not allow enough time to hold fair tryouts, teach basic skills, and prepare a team for the season. In such cases, you must find time during the summer to evaluate your incoming athletes and to involve yourself in a program where you can teach and incorporate your philosophies. Evaluating players and teaching the major points should be completed before the spring season begins. To maximize your preseason practices, know your personnel before you begin.

If your state rules committee or school permits, you should hold games during the fall to give you opportunity to evaluate and teach. If this is impossible, you will have to evaluate your players during any summer involvement and/or spring drills and do the best you can in the time available. Using time to evaluate talent of course cuts down on the quality time you need to develop your players. If you must evaluate during the spring, never give up time allotted for drills to stop and teach basic skills. If teaching basic skills must be done in the spring, divide the group and accomplish this in a separate area, such as in a classroom, on a stage, or in a hallway, while drills are going on in the basic skills area.

Prioritizing Your Players

Once the evaluation of available talent is complete, your next goal is to determine who will be given top priority during practice drills and situations. The players projected to play the most during the coming season should be involved in the greatest number of available repetitions.

Pitchers.   Prioritizing your pitching staff will depend on the rotation. Those likely to start during the season should be top priority when it comes to building endurance. We like to take eight pitchers and build their endurance from 100 to

120 pitches over a period of 7 to 8 weeks. We develop our relievers with fewer repetitions—anywhere from 75 to 100 pitches.

Catchers, Infielders, and Outfielders.   The top catchers should handle the top pitchers. The advanced infielders should work with the most developed outfielders. During drills, try to have at least two players at each position. This allows you to control who is working with whom and gives the players involved time to rest.

Hitters.   When prioritizing hitters, your toughest decision is in determining how many batters can receive adequate hitting experience in a given day. Based on the time limits for most teams, you may be lucky to give 12 to 14 hitters the quality number of contacts or at-bats necessary to adequately develop their hitting.

As you prioritize your hitting, keep in mind your batting order. Those most likely to hit during games should receive priority batting time. These are the players that need the repetitions. Our goal is to get the top 14 hitters the quality repetitions they need to be successful. Those less likely to play get fewer.

SCHEDULING PRACTICE

The most difficult time to run practice is during the preseason. Most teams are confined by time restraints and are usually battling other athletic teams and extracurricular groups for use of the facilities. As you focus your attention on scheduling practice, keep in mind that your practices should simulate game situations as much as possible—this includes all drillwork, baserunning, pitching, hitting, and team defense.

In developing a preseason practice schedule, focus on the number of weeks and days before the first game. In scheduling practices and determining what needs to be accomplished, work backward from the first game (see Figure 3.1). This is the date that all of your practices should be targeting. All possible game situations must be simulated before your first game.

Assuming you do not have the luxury of 7 to 8 preseason practice weeks to prepare your team, it is best to adjust your practice schedule to best fit the needs of your team, players, and coaching philosophy. Such adjustments may mean

- finding another space to hold practice,
- holding practice at night, taking advantage of the most time and space, or
- bringing in a select number of players on a certain day to develop their skills.

Sunday	Monday	Tuesday	Wednesday	Thursday	Friday	Saturday
12	13 Drill work—week long	14	15	16	17	18
19	20 Drill work—week long	21	22	23	24	25
26	27 Man on (1st)	28 Man on (1st)	29 Man on (2nd)	30 Man on (2nd)	31 Practice games	1 Practice games
2 Practice games	3 Man on (3rd)	4 Man on (3rd)	5 Men on (1st & 3rd)	6 Men on (1st & 3rd)	7 Practice games	8 Practice games
9 Practice games	10 Men on (1st), (2nd)	11 Men on (1st), (2nd)	12 Man on (3rd) (1st & 3rd)	13 Man on (3rd) (1st & 3rd)	14 Practice games	15 Practice games
16	17 Review	18 Review	19 Review	20 Review	21 Season opener	22
23	24	25	26	27	28	1
2	3	4	5	6	7	

Figure 3.1 A sample defense practice schedule for the weeks leading up to the season opener.

Coach's Corner

I remember holding a practice game at 4:30 a.m. one Sunday because my facilities would not be available to me that day. It was critical that four pitchers stay on their throwing schedule. I knew that everyone wanted to sleep in, but for the good of the team, we had to practice. Mike Leblanc, eventually drafted by Seattle, and Steve Loubier, drafted by California, had to increase their endurance from 90 to 105 pitches. Every player was ready to stretch at 4 a.m. and the game was finished by 7. After Dale Plummer, now with the New York Mets, and Marc Powers finished their relief duty, I walked into the training room and found Mike and Steve asleep as they iced their arms.

As you begin to cover different aspects of indoor practice sessions, don't forget the emphasis of priority planning as you maximize quality time and limited space. Keep in mind that your athletes must be in good physical condition so that they will be able to devote their time and attention to fine-tuning their baseball skills. Attempt to follow your overall practice schedule in preparing for the season.

- Develop sessions that are best for the most possible players and that focus on the purpose of each day's practice.
- Make sure that those who will play regularly get the required repetitions at bat and in the field.
- Keep your pitchers on rotation. Do not make so many changes that you affect the confidence of your players.

PART II Practice by Position

Once you have finished setting priorities and planning to make the most of your space and time, you're ready to hold practice. Transferring your plans from paper to practice, however, doesn't happen automatically. You now face unique challenges as you begin training your players for their individual positions.

Orchestrating how each player rotates through each practice station is difficult. The practice needs of catchers differ from those of outfielders, just as starting pitchers need different training than their relievers do. It is also important that your main players receive adequate repetitions of skills and that your reserve players aren't left out. All this requires careful planning.

In Part II we show you how to schedule your practices efficiently. We offer drills that keep sessions moving and eliminate situations where players are standing around. In our drills we consider the role of each position as it relates to the team, as well as the skills needed to play the position successfully. For each drill we outline our objectives, the skills the drill emphasizes, how to set up and perform the drill, and our own coaching tips. When appropriate, we offer variations to add diversity to your practice and to help you adapt to special circumstances you might encounter.

In each chapter we analyze and offer several practice sessions to help you meet your goals based on the plans and priorities you outlined prior to preseason practice. We've included 28 illustrated, easy-to-understand drills for pitchers, catchers, infielders, and outfielders. We show you how to prioritize the drills to meet your needs. From mastering the double-play to fielding the bunt, these drills show you how to get the most for your players out of each practice session. A unique feature of the drills is that they can all be performed either outdoors or indoors, so you're not restricted by changing climates.

As you read through Part II, keep in mind the unique aspects of your practice situations. We do not use all of the drills that appear here at Maine. Some fit our needs better than others. Examine each drill carefully to determine how you can use it in your practice sessions, or consider ways to adapt the drill based on the make-up of your team and the time and space you have available.

As we said in Part I, our top priority at Maine is developing the endurance of our pitchers. However, to be successful, pitchers must combine proper mechanics with endurance. In addition to the four pitcher drills in chapter 4, we include our 6-step warm-up drill, which stresses endurance and proper technique for pitching a baseball safely and effectively. We'll begin Part II with tips for holding practice for pitchers.

CHAPTER 4

Pitchers

If you look back through the years of baseball at the high school, college, and professional levels, you'll find that the key for championship teams has been a talented and deep pitching staff. If your pitchers consistently throw good strikes to location without giving the hitter the fat of the bat, your team should have a shot at being one of those championship teams.

Coach's Corner

Many of the great teams I have had at Maine have been deep in pitching. In the early 1980s, Billy Swift and Joe Johnson led our team to four college world series appearances. In the mid-1980s, Scott Morse, Jeff Plympton, and Steve Loubier led us to the college world series. In the late 1980s and early 1990s, Mike D'Andrea, Larry Thomas, and Ben Burlingame helped establish a team record 48 wins in one season. What has worked for us before is still working for us today: We still rely on good old-fashioned pitching to win games.

Pitchers cannot win on talent alone. They must learn proper mechanics. They must be carefully handled so as not to overstress their pitching arms. You can increase a pitcher's chance for success by teaching proper mechanics and developing endurance cautiously.

Like any aspect of baseball, pitching requires careful planning, endless practice, and proper mechanics to become consistent enough to win ballgames. In developing practice sessions for pitchers, focus on three important areas:

- Proper pitching mechanics
- Building endurance (based on a 4-day pitching rotation)
- Providing live pitching opportunities so the pitcher can establish and routinely handle a strike zone

We'll discuss each of these aspects in depth in the sections that follow.

MASTERING PROPER MECHANICS

A pitcher must master proper mechanics to help protect himself from injury. Although as a coach you cannot provide a pitcher complete safety from injury, you can certainly reduce the chances. Proper pitching mechanics also make for consistency. As a pitcher becomes consistent in his routine and delivery, he is likely to also be consistent in throwing strikes.

Coach's Corner

I once had a pitcher who threw comfortably in the low- to mid-80s but who could not consistently throw strikes. For 2 years he was a mediocre pitcher—and then he perfected his delivery. By the middle of his junior year, he was our number-1 pitcher and was clocked at 94 mph by a Major League scout. Later he was drafted into professional baseball.

When developing proper pitching mechanics, focus on a routine to achieve and emphasize the important aspects of delivering a pitch and protecting the arm and rotator cuff. One way to accomplish this is through implementing a step-by-step routine, while monitoring the pitcher's endurance. At Maine, we have developed such a routine that isolates the pitcher's mechanics and simultaneously builds his endurance through 6 steps.

The 6-Step Warm-Up Routine

The 6-step routine allows a pitcher to carefully warm up while slowly increasing the distance between each step. Each step is a new drill that focuses on an aspect of pitching mechanics, making the pitcher's delivery more consistent. The drill also serves as a starting point in building endurance.

These are the five goals of the 6-step routine:

- To allow the pitcher to safely stretch out while concentrating on specific mechanics
- To develop a routine for the pitcher to properly warm up
- To practice and make a habit of using proper pitching mechanics
- To allow 10 repetitions in each step that focus on certain aspects of the pitcher's delivery (with each step in the progression relying on each of the earlier steps)
- To complete, in 15 to 20 minutes, the progression in which the pitcher gradually works back to the full distance of 60 feet, 6 inches

STEP 1

TWO-KNEE DRILL

Goal.   To synchronize the travel of the arm and elbow with that of the shoulder and hip to ensure proper follow-through.

Equipment.   A baseball, a mat or soft surface to kneel on.

Procedure.   The pitcher kneels about 15 ft from and squared to the catcher (Figure 4.1a). With the ball in his throwing hand, the pitcher rotates his upper body so that his nonthrowing shoulder and elbow points to the catcher (Figure 4.1b) as he brings his throwing arm and the ball up to the cocked position

(Figure 4.1c). Once the arm and hand are in the cocked position, the pitcher gains momentum by uncoiling his upper body. He then spins the ball at half-speed to a location as he stretches out. As the pitcher releases the ball, he protects his arm and shoulder with the proper follow-through—armpit over the knee, elbow by the knee, and a complete sweep of the fingers (Figure 4.1d).

Note. At this stage, the best location to develop is low and inside to the opposite hitter—right-handed pitchers to left-handed hitters, and vice versa.

Figure 4.1a

Figure 4.1b

Figure 4.1c

Figure 4.1d

STEP 2 *ONE-KNEE DRILL*

Goals.   (1) To develop a perfect stride location in which the knee and toe are pointed in the direction of the catcher. (2) To establish a correct and consistent path of the arm. (3) To ensure a proper follow-through where the armpit is over the knee, the elbow by the knee, and the hip rotating toward the catcher to ensure proper drive toward the plate.

Equipment.   A baseball, a mat or soft surface to kneel on.

Procedure.   The pitcher and catcher position themselves about 20 feet apart. The pitcher kneels on his drive-leg knee with his stride leg bent toward the catcher. Ensure that the stride leg (or landing leg) is in the ideal landing position: out in front of the body, which is squared facing the catcher. Most of the pitcher's weight should be over his kneeling leg. With the ball in his throwing hand, the pitcher rotates his upper body, so that his nonthrowing shoulder and elbow point toward the catcher, and raises his throwing arm and hand through the correct arm path and to the cocked position (Figure 4.2a). While in the cocked position, the pitcher focuses on location. As he throws, he transfers his weight from the back leg to the front leg by pushing off the back foot, raising from a kneeling to standing position, while uncoiling his upper body to allow for the explosion and travel of the arm, elbow, shoulder, and hip. Again, as the pitcher releases the ball, he must concentrate on the proper follow-through—armpit over the knee, elbow by the knee, sweep of the fingers, and rotation of the hips (Figure 4.2b).

Figure 4.2a

Figure 4.2b

STEP 3

HIP OR CHAIR DRILL

Goals. (1) To develop quickness of the arm coming down and out of the glove. (2) To focus on the powerful rotation of the hip to gain momentum toward home plate.

Equipment. A baseball, a pitcher's mound or a folding chair, tape or chalk to mark the landing point.

Procedure. The pitcher stands on the mound about 30 ft from the catcher. The pitcher needs to measure off his stride line, ensuring his toe and knee are pointing toward the catcher. (Remember—the stride foot and knee are the guide for momentum and the path of the arm.) The pitcher begins with his hands at break point (Figure 4.3a). This is the point where the hand and glove separate as the pitcher brings his throwing hand down and out of the glove and into cocked position (Figure 4.3b). As the arm nears the cocked position, most of the pitcher's weight will be over his drive leg. Once the pitcher is at cocked position, he will simultaneously transfer his weight from the drive leg to the front leg, begin rotation of the hips toward the catcher, and bring the arm and shoulder through the proper throwing path, ending with the correct follow-through (Figure 4.3c).

Note. This drill develops powerful hip rotation. Upon follow-through, the pitcher should not bring his drive foot forward. He merely turns the foot over so that the outside part of the ankle points toward the ground and the inside of the knee toward the opposite knee.

Figure 4.3a

Figure 4.3b

Figure 4.3c

Figure 4.4a

The chair drill uses the same ideas and concepts as the hip drill but may be used when a mound is unavailable. Use the chair to simulate the mound's downward slope.

Procedure.   As with the hip drill, the chair drill requires the pitcher and catcher to be about 30 ft apart. The pitcher measures his stride and places his push-off foot on the seat of the chair (Figure 4.4a). With his hands at break point, the pitcher pulls the ball down and out of the glove and into the cocked position (Figure 4.4b). At this point, most of his weight should be over his drive leg. From the cocked position, the pitcher simultaneously transfers his weight from the drive leg to the front leg, begins rotation of the hips, and brings his arm and shoulder through the proper throwing path, ending with the correct follow-through (Figure 4.4c).

Note.   The push-off foot does not leave the chair. The pitcher should concentrate on turning the foot over and rotating the hip. His weight should not shift forward until his arm is up and in the cocked position.

Figure 4.4b

Figure 4.4c

STEP
4 | BALANCE POINT DRILL

Goals.   (1) To line the pitcher's body to gain momentum toward home plate. (2) To develop a consistent arm motion through a proper stride.

Equipment.   A baseball, a pitcher's mound, tape or chalk to mark the landing point.

Procedure.   This step, along with Steps 5 and 6, should be done from the pitcher's mound. The catcher positions himself about 45 ft away from the pitcher. The pitcher marks the point at which his stride foot should land. This makes it easier for you to verify a correct landing spot.

With all of his weight over his drive leg, the pitcher raises his stride leg until his thigh is parallel to the ground (Figure 4.5a). The stride toe should be pointed down to allow the pitcher to land on the front half of his foot. The glove and throwing hand should be at break point. The pitcher focuses on the catcher's mitt, breaks his throwing hand down and out of the glove and brings it quickly to the cocked position. At the same time, he strides toward the plate, transferring his weight from the back to the front leg, begins hip rotation, and brings his drive foot off the ground and forward as he moves his arm and shoulder through the proper throwing path. He should end with the correct follow-through (Figure 4.5b).

Notes.   Unlike in the chair or hip drill, the pitcher should rotate his drive foot so that the outside part of the ankle is pointing toward the catcher and the heel is pointing toward the appropriate base. A right-handed pitcher's heel will point toward third base and a left-handed pitcher's heel toward first.

To ensure proper arm protection, make sure the pitching arm is brought quickly to the cocked position before the pitcher shifts his weight and gains momentum toward home plate. Before cocking his arm, the pitcher focuses on the catcher's mitt. The stride toe and knee must point in the direction of the catcher. In the follow-through, the outside part of the ankle should point toward the catcher and the heel toward the appropriate base.

Figure 4.5a

Figure 4.5b

STEP
5

ONE, TWO, THREE DRILL

Goals. (1) To bring together Steps 1 through 4. (2) To break the delivery into three stages, stopping after each stage to ensure that the pitcher is in the correct position. Stage 1 focuses on addressing the rubber and beginning the delivery. Stage 2 emphasizes the balance point. Stage 3 concentrates on the release of the ball.

Equipment. A baseball, a pitcher's mound.

Procedure. The catcher positions himself about 50 ft from the pitcher. In Stage 1 of this drill, the pitcher addresses the rubber, gaining momentum by stepping back with his stride leg and turning his pivot foot in front of the rubber. As he begins this rocking step, it is important for him to keep both his wrist and the ball completely hidden in his glove. At this point, the pitcher should stop and check his position (Figure 4.6a).

Stage 2 concentrates on the balance point and cocked position (Figure 4.6b). As the pitcher reaches the balance point, make sure his wrist and the ball are concealed from the batter's view. Remember to stop at this phase to check that the pitcher is in proper balance, with hands breaking from the middle of his body to go to cocked position.

Stage 3 is the throwing and follow-through stage. With arm in the cocked position and weight over his back leg, the pitcher aims his hip and front shoulder toward the target. He drives with the back leg and strides toward the plate. As the stride foot lands, he transfers his weight from the back leg to the front leg, rotates his upper body so that the throwing shoulder replaces the nonthrowing shoulder, opens his hip toward the catcher, brings his arm and shoulder through the proper throwing path, and ends with the correct follow-through (Figure 4.6c).

Figure 4.6a

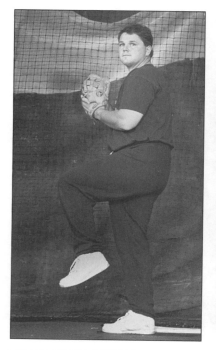

Figure 4.6b

Figure 4.6c

STEP 6 STRETCH DRILL

Figure 4.7a

Goals.   (1) To develop the slide step to minimize its effect on proper pitching mechanics. (2) To shorten the leg kick to quicken the delivery home. (3) To ensure the arm is in the cocked position before gaining momentum in the throwing direction.

Equipment.   A baseball, a pitching mound.

Procedure.   The stretch is from full distance, 60 ft, 6 in. In developing the slide step, the pitcher is to quicken his delivery home while least influencing his proper pitching mechanics. From the stretch, the pitcher comes to set position (Figure 4.7a). His feet are a little more than shoulder-width apart, and his weight is evenly distributed. As he breaks his hands down and out of the glove and up to cocked position, his weight transfers to the drive leg (Figures 4.7b and c). This places him in the cocked or power position. As he begins his delivery home, he lifts his stride leg enough to gain momentum and steps toward home. After completing the stride, he transfers his weight from his back leg to front leg, begins rotation of the upper body and hips, brings his arm and shoulder through the proper throwing path, and ends in the correct follow-through position (Figure 4.7d).

Once Step 6 is completed, the pitcher should be adequately warm and stretched. He is now ready for the rest of his throwing experience, whether it is his long or short throwing day. At this point, gradually add other pitches to the fastball, such as the curve, slider, or change. Once he is comfortable with his pitches, let him complete his throwing for that day.

Figure 4.7b

Figure 4.7c

Figure 4.7d

BUILDING ENDURANCE

Developing endurance and carefully monitoring your pitcher are as important as having proper mechanics. Like any athlete in training, it takes time for a pitcher to develop the muscles required to throw a baseball. For programs at the college level, we've found that pitchers can safely build endurance in 7 to 8 weeks. This allows enough time to build their endurance to the point that they can throw 100 pitches every 4 or 5 days.

Because of the restrictions in most high school programs, high school coaches are lucky to have 4 weeks to prepare their teams for the approaching season. Even if you are restricted to 3, 4, or 5 weeks, it is critical that you do not rush your pitchers.

High school coaches might find that their best pitchers are also the best athletes on the team. When they are not pitching, they are playing another position, often in the infield. They may pitch one day, play shortstop the next, and then come back and pitch a day or two later. Often coaches start a player at a position and then bring him in to pitch if needed. This type of use places undue stress on the pitcher's shoulder and elbow. It is not uncommon for such a pitcher to become arm tired, develop bad habits, and injure himself.

If you want to use pitchers as everyday players, play them in the outfield or use them as a designated hitter (DH). To safely develop pitchers, you must treat them as pitchers. You will get more mileage and have more success by developing and maintaining a healthy pitching staff.

Your focus in building a pitcher's endurance is to

- safely progress him to the point that he can comfortably throw 100 pitches,
- develop appropriate speed for the pitching stage, and
- prepare him for the demands of game day.

The safest and most effective way to build endurance is on a 4-day rotation. Remember—our goal is to slowly build endurance while concentrating on proper mechanics and location.

The 4-Day Rotation

The 4-day rotation was designed to give the pitcher adequate rest between long throwing experiences and to be used as a guide in developing pitcher endurance (see Table 4.1). By following the 4-day rotation, you will afford your pitchers the appropriate rest while building their endurance.

Day 1. The first day is the long throwing or endurance day. On this day, emphasize adding pitches to your pitcher's throwing experience. For example, if your pitcher threw 60 pitches on his last long throwing experience, he should throw 75 pitches on his current long throwing experience and 90 on his next long throwing experience. Begin counting the number of pitches thrown once your pitcher is warmed up (use our 6-step warm-up routine).

Day 2. The second day is conditioning day and always follows the long throwing day. This day is used as a conditioning and pitcher's drill day. On this day the pitcher will work hard to help get his arm and legs back into shape.

Day 3. The third day is for short throwing. This is a stretch throwing day. Once the pitcher has completed the 6-step warm-up routine, he throws 12 to 15 pitches from full distance. He should concentrate on proper mechanics and location.

Table 4.1	THE 4-DAY ROTATION		
Long day	**Conditioning day**	**Short day**	**Rest day**
1. Endurance pitching experience 2. Endurance running	1. Endurance running 2. Interval running 3. Weight training 4. Pappas routine 5. Two-ball 6. Fielding drills	1. Short throw 2. Endurance running 3. Fielding drills	1. Light throwing 2. Endurance running 3. Interval running 4. Pappas routine 5. Two-ball 6. Fielding drills

Day 4. The fourth day is a rest day, with no live throwing to a catcher. The pitcher may play some light toss to stretch his arm, but that is the extent of the throwing.

The 4-day rotation is designed to allow adequate rest for your pitchers. Here are some other guidelines to follow:

- If your pitcher throws 60 or more pitches, he should have at least 3 days of rest before the next long throwing experience.
- If he throws between 45 and 60 pitches in a day, the pitcher should have 2 days of rest from long throwing. The 45 to 60 pitch range is a gray area. The more pitches thrown, the more rest needed.
- If your pitcher throws fewer than 45 pitches, he should have at least 1 day of rest before throwing again.

Know the strength and recovery times of your pitchers. The longer it takes a pitcher to recover, the more rest he will need between long throwing experiences. Setting guidelines for your pitchers will benefit the team in the long run.

Knowledge of your preseason timetable is essential in developing your pitching staff. The length of preseason—3, 4, 5, or 7 weeks—will dictate the timetable of development for your pitchers. The more time you have, the more developed your starting pitchers will be before the first game. The shorter your preseason, the more important your relievers become because your starters will not be able to go as long. In such cases, you will be developing your starting pitchers as the season progresses.

Pitcher Progression

Improper mechanics can lead to arm problems and injuries. The same is true of overuse and improper handling of pitchers. To give your pitcher the greatest amount of protection from injury, monitor his endurance progression during the preseason. This will ensure that pitchers have adequate rest between outings and afford them the protection they need.

One way to monitor your pitchers' endurance is by following a progression chart (see pages 35-39). In developing a pitcher progression chart, you need to know the roles of each pitcher before the season begins. You will want to know who your starters, middle relievers, and closers are going to be. Their roles on the team will be your guide to the building of their endurance. In developing a progression chart, focus on the game-day routine. The long day should be used to increase endurance through live pitching and hitting. For the pitcher, this should continue every fourth day until each pitcher raises his pitch count to the desired total.

Starting pitchers require the most time because you want to build their endurance to 100+ pitches. At 15 pitches every 4 days, this is going to take some time. The middle relievers and closers require less time. Their pitch count will take less time as middle relievers build pitch endurance in the 45 to 60 pitch range and closers in the 45 to 50 range.

Once each pitcher's role is decided, you will need to develop four groups for the rotation to be effective. There should be two starters or long relievers in each group, and then fill in the remaining slots with middle relievers and closers. Table 4.2 provides an example of a group listing. The top two names in each group are starters and long relievers. The last two names are middle relievers and closers.

Table 4.2	A 4-GROUP PITCHING ROTATION		
Group 1	**Group 2**	**Group 3**	**Group 4**
Hanning	Ballard	Bogardus	Smith
Baressi	Dryswak	Cassidy	Coombs
Decker	Foran	Jones	Lucas
Allen	Veilleux	Quinn	Trundy

7-Week Pitch Progression.   The 7-week progression allows for full development of all of your pitchers (see Figure 4.8).

Week 1 is used as a stretch week. All pitchers are to use the 6-step routine until they are back to full distance. Once a pitcher is at full distance, he throws the required number of pitches. All pitchers involved in the program will throw the first 5 days. The number of pitches thrown increases each day, as shown:

- Day 1—the pitcher throws 4 pitches
- Day 2—7 pitches
- Day 3—10 pitches
- Day 4—13 pitches
- Day 5—17 pitches

	Sunday	Monday	Tuesday	Wednesday	Thursday	Friday	Saturday
January vacation; stretching at home	5	6 Short day	7	8 Long day	9	10 Short day	11
6-step stretch week	12 Stretch to distance (60 ft, 6 in.) 4 pitches	13 7 pitches	14 All groups 10 pitches	15 13 pitches	16 17 pitches	17 Groups 1 & 3 B.P. round 13 pitches (1/2-speed)	18 Groups 2 & 4 B.P. round 13 pitches (1/2-speed)
Batting practice week; rotation starts	19 Groups 1 & 3 Batting practice 20 pitches (1/2-speed)	20 Groups 2 & 4 Batting practice 20 pitches (1/2-speed)	21 Groups 1 & 3 Batting practice 26 pitches (1/2-speed)	22 Groups 2 & 4 Batting practice 26 pitches (1/2-speed)	23 Group 1 13p (1/2-speed) 13p (3/4-speed)	24 Group 2 13p (1/2-speed) 13p (3/4-speed)	25 Group 3 13p (1/2-speed) 13p (3/4-speed)
Rotation live hitting	26 Group 4 13p (1/2-speed) 13p (3/4-speed)	27 Group 1 15p (3/4-speed) 15p (full speed)	28 Group 2	29 Group 3	30 Group 4	31 Group 1 39 pitches 13F 13F	1 Group 2
	2 Group 3	3 Group 4	4 Group 1 45 pitches 15F 15F 15F	5 Group 2	6 Group 3	7 Group 4	8 Group 1 Indoor game 60 pitches 4 sets of 15
	9 Group 2	10 Group 3	11 Group 4	12 Group 1 75 pitches 15-15-15-15 F	13 Group 2	14 Group 3	15 Group 4
	16 Group 1 Indoor game 90 pitches 6 sets of 15	17 Group 2	18 Group 3	19 Group 4	20 Group 1 Indoor game 105 pitches 7 sets of 15	21 Group 2	22 Group 3
	23 Group 4	24 Group 1 Indoor game 120 pitches 8 sets of 15	25 Group 2	26 Group 3	27 Group 4	28 Group 1 vs. LSU	29 Group 2 vs. LSU
	1 Group 3 vs. LSU	2 Group 4 vs. UNO	3	4	5	6	7

Figure 4.8   A pitcher's 7-week progression chart.

35

Each day, after he has completed the required pitches, it is important for the pitcher to cool down. The cool-down will vary from day to day. On day 1, from half-distance (30 feet) and at half-speed, he should throw two sets of spins, including forward (the spin of a fastball), backward (a curve spin), and change (the spin of a change-up). As a cool-down on day 2, he will throw three sets of spins, on day 3, he'll throw 4 sets of spins, and so on until he finishes day 5 of practice. As he spins the ball to the catcher, he must concentrate on proper mechanics and stretching.

The next 4 days are reserved for batting practice rounds. During this stage, the pitchers begin to throw to live batters. Here, our goal is to develop both the pitchers and the hitters. The schedule for batting practice pitching is as follows:

- Day 1—pitching groups 1 and 3 throw 13 pitches at half-speed while standing behind a protective screen. Each pitch is thrown down the middle of the strike zone.

- Day 2—repeat day 1 with pitchers from groups 2 and 4.

- Day 3—groups 1 and 3 throw 20 pitches at half-speed.

- Day 4—groups 3 and 4 throw 20 pitches at half-speed.

This continues until all groups have thrown 26 pitches during the batting practice rounds. Once this is completed, the 4-day rotation begins.

The goal of rotation and each pitching experience is twofold. First, the pitcher must master the strike zone and concentrate on mechanics. Second, the pitcher will increase the number of pitches thrown every fourth day through game experiences. Looking at Figure 4.8, you see that rotation begins on the 12th day of practice. On the first day of rotation, each pitcher scheduled in Group 1 throws two innings of 13 pitches. The first inning is at half-speed and the second inning at three-quarter speed. Pitchers throw eight fastballs, three curveballs, and two change-ups. The last five pitches are from the stretch.

On the first day of rotation, Group 2 has its conditioning day; Group 3, its short throwing day; and Group 4, its rest day. All groups then continue in their respective 4-day cycles.

On the 16th day of practice, Group 1 engages in another long throwing experience. Each long experience is designed like a game, with varying numbers of innings. The schedule for the 16th day includes two innings. In each inning, the number of pitches increases to 15 (eight fastballs, four curves, three change-ups, six from the stretch). The first inning's pitches are at three-quarter speed, and the second inning's at full speed. The other groups repeat this increase on their long throwing days.

To build endurance and strength, the number of pitches thrown on the long throwing day increases by 15 pitches each time. Have your pitchers throw these extra 15 pitches at only half- to three-quarter speed, and continue with this progression until they have reached the desired number of pitches for their role. Starting pitchers and long relievers will progress to 120 pitches. Middle relievers will work in the 80 to 100 pitch range and closers will work in the 45 to 60 pitch range.

5- and 4-Week Pitch Progressions.   Having less time to develop your pitchers means you have to develop more pitchers that can throw longer. In the case of having 4 or 5 weeks to prepare, your starters will be able to throw 60 to 90 pitches, depending on the routine. In the 5-week progression, your starting pitchers and long relievers should be able to throw in the 70 to 80 pitch range. In 4 weeks, they should be able to throw in the 60 to 70 pitch range. This should get you through only four or five innings. Consequently, you need to have more pitchers prepared to get you through the game (see Figures 4.9 and 4.10). As the

	Sunday	Monday	Tuesday	Wednesday	Thursday	Friday	Saturday
6-step stretch week		**12** 7 pitches	**13** Stretch to distance (60 ft, 6 in.) 10 pitches	**14** 13 pitches	**15** 17 pitches	**16** Rest	**17** B.P. round 13p (1/2-speed)
	18	**19** 13 pitches (1/2-speed) 13 pitches (3/4-speed)	**20**	**21** 13 pitches (3/4-speed) 13 pitches (full speed)	**22**	**23** Short throwing day	**24**
	25 15 (full speed)	**26**	**27** Short day	**28**	**29** 30 pitches (F) 15-15	**30**	**1**
	2	**3** 45 pitches 15-15-15	**4**	**5** Short day	**6**	**7** 60 pitches 15-15-15-15	**8**
	9 Short day	**10**	**11** 75 pitches 15-15-15-15-15	**12**	**13** Short day	**14**	**15** Game 75 to 90 pitches

Figure 4.9 A pitcher's 5-week progression chart.

Sunday	Monday	Tuesday	Wednesday	Thursday	Friday	Saturday
	12 10 pitches	**13** Stretch to distance (60 ft, 6 in.) 13 pitches	**14** 17 pitches	**15** Rest	**16** B.P. round 13p (1/2-speed) 13p (3/4-speed)	**17**
18 13 pitches (3/4-speed) 13 pitches (full speed)	**19**	**20** Short day	**21**	**22** 15 pitches (full speed)	**23**	**24** Short day
25	**26** 30 pitches 15-15	**27**	**28** Short day	**29**	**30** 45 pitches 15-15-15	**1**
2 Short day	**3**	**4** 60 pitches 15-15-15-15	**5**	**6** Short day	**7**	**8** Game 60 to 75 pitches

Figure 4.10 A pitcher's 4-week progression chart.

season continues and pitchers build endurance, your starters and long relievers will be able to throw more pitches.

A short preseason places a great deal of responsibility on the coach. You must not rush your pitchers by preparing them too quickly. Pushing them to pitch more than they are ready for will cause harm in the long run. Once the season begins, use a pitch count and follow it closely. Remember that you are dealing with young men who are still developing physically.

Coaches in programs with practice limitations will have to develop a pitcher progression chart to suit their available time and space. When developing your chart, it is important to keep your pitchers on the 4-day rotation. This may mean that a pitcher will be scheduled to throw on Sunday, which is against regulations in many states. In such a case, you will have to find a way for the pitcher to legally and safely get his work in. More on this later.

Practice Schedules

At Maine, we use about 16 pitchers each season. Due to the demand of our competitive schedule and the number of games we play, we want to make sure that we have enough quality pitching to get us through the season.

Our philosophy is to develop eight starters and eight relievers in a 7- to 8-week period. With a 56-game regular season, we must have this many pitchers ready to compete. Those of you who have 15- to 20-game schedules over 8 weeks may be able to get by with fewer pitchers. It's very important to have enough pitchers prepared to get you through the season.

To use your time efficiently, you should prepare daily, weekly, and monthly practice schedules. When doing so, focus each practice session on your philosophy of pitching. Make sure your players know their responsibilities for practice on each day and over the course of a week. If players know their weekly and daily practice schedules, they can prepare beforehand. Then you won't have to waste practice time explaining responsibilities.

Pitchers' Monthly Practice Schedule. Use the pitcher preseason endurance progression schedule as your monthly guide. The chart will help you in developing weekly and daily practice schedules and in preparing your pitchers for the season. Once you've completed a general outline of your pitcher progression chart, understanding and developing the weekly and daily practice schedules will be much easier.

Pitchers' Weekly Practice Schedule. As you develop a weekly pitcher practice chart, keep in mind the rules and regulations of your school, league, and state that will influence the development of your schedules. Many states prohibit high schoolers from practicing on Sunday. If this is your situation, and if you have a pitcher on the 4-day rotation, his endurance day and short throwing day will be every other Sunday. You will need to have your pitcher fulfill his throwing requirements under safe and legal guidelines. If he understands the weekly pitcher schedule, he can plan ahead of time. It is important to always have an adult supervising when the coach cannot be (or is not allowed to be) present.

In our system at Maine, practice week runs Monday through Sunday. We implement and practice drills Monday through Thursday and use them in game situations Friday through Sunday. Our weekly practice chart appears in Table 4.3. At the top of each day is the group involved in endurance pitching. During this particular week, Group 1 will throw long on Monday and Friday. Group 2 will throw long on Tuesday and Saturday, Group 3 on Wednesday and

Sunday, and Group 4 on Thursday and Monday of the eighth day. On a particular day, the number of pitches that group will throw should be placed under the group number. Monday through Thursday, each group throws 45 pitches. The number increases to 60 pitches on Friday. The pitchers not involved in endurance throwing should follow their routine outlined in the 4-day rotation.

Table 4.3	THE PITCHERS' WEEKLY PRACTICE SCHEDULE					
Monday	**Tuesday**	**Wednesday**	**Thursday**	**Friday**	**Saturday**	**Sunday**
Group 1	**Group 2**	**Group 3**	**Group 4**	**Group 1**	**Group 2**	**Group 3**
Endurance 45 pitches	Endurance 45 pitches	Endurance 45 pitches	Endurance 45 pitches	Endurance 60 pitches	Endurance 60 pitches	Endurance 60 pitches
Pitcher drills	Pitcher drills	Pitcher drills	Pitcher drills	Game	Game	Game
Situation: Man on 1st	Situation: Man on 1st	Situation: Men on 1st and 2nd	Situation: Men on 1st and 2nd			

After endurance pitching has been covered, the routine for group work should be scheduled next. Monday through Thursday, all pitchers involved in the program participate in pitcher drills and situation play. In this case, situations with a man on first will be covered on Monday and Tuesday, situations with men on first and second will be covered Wednesday and Thursday, and Friday through Sunday are left for practice games. If your facilities don't accommodate practice games, you need to adjust your practice session to keep your pitchers on schedule.

Pitchers' Daily Practice Schedule. Daily practice schedules keep your practices running smoothly and your players involved. When players understand their daily responsibilities, practice becomes efficient and focused. We believe in keeping all players involved in practice at all times. While pitchers do pitcher drills, outfielders may be hitting off the tees.

Tables 4.4 and 4.5 outline a daily practice session. Table 4.4 shows the time frame and responsibilities of the players involved in drills. These drills take place in the basic skills area. Pitchers are involved in pitcher drills from 3:00 to 3:10. During this period, they practice throws to each base, covering first, squeeze plays, wild-pitch drills, and holding runners on. From 3:10 to 3:50, they learn how to cover bunt, steal, rundown, and batted-ball situations with a runner on first.

Table 4.5 outlines the responsibilities of all pitchers and players involved in live pitching and hitting. This takes place in the designated pitching and hitting area. This particular schedule assumes that the pitching and hitting area has two cages. If your pitching and hitting area has only one cage, a different chart should be used.

In the outline shown, the time frame of each sequence is in the left-hand corner. Each session designates an inning. The first inning begins at 4:00 and runs to 4:08. The second inning runs from 4:08 to 4:16, and so on, until the required innings have been fulfilled. The pitchers (P) designated for assign-

Table 4.4	A DAILY PRACTICE SCHEDULE		

Infield area

Time	Activity	Time	Activity
2:50	Team stretching	3:30	Defense versus rundown, runner at first
3:00	Pitcher drills: D'Andrea, Novio, Nadeau, Thomas, Dryswak, Hewes, Beaudet, Dillon, Johnson A. Throw to first, second, and third B. Cover first, squeeze, squeeze C. Wild pitch D. Holding runners	3:40	Defense versus batted ball, Little League
		3:50	Square drill: Delucia Knox Seguin Scott Sweeney Tate Slicer Hartung Johnson Small Wild Wilson Beal Duff Tall Kelliher
		4:00	Outfield drills: Sweeney, White, Beal, Lucas
3:10	Defense versus bunt, runner at first	4:10	Infield drills: Knox Seguin Delucia Scott Slicer Willey Thompson Trundy
3:20	Defense versus steal, runner at first	4:30	Bunting, baserunning

Table 4.5	A DAILY SCHEDULE FOR LIVE PITCHING AND HITTING	

Area 1	Area 2
4:00 **P** Higgins (15) **B** Thomas **C** Kelliher **H** Knox, Seguin, Scott	4:00 **P** Burlingame (15) **B** Dryswak **C** Ender **H** Delucia, Hartung, Slicer
4:08 **P** Brenner (15) **B** Smith **C** Thrasher **H** Knox, Seguin, Scott	4:08 **P** Dillon (15) **B** Therrien **C** King **H** Delucia, Hartung, Slicer
4:16 **P** Burlingame (15) **B** D'Andrea **C** Delaney **H** White, Kelliher, Tobin	4:16 **P** Higgins (15) **B** Hewes **C** Taylor **H** Sweeney, Ender, Phillips
4:24 **P** Dillon (15) **B** Brown **C** Tobin **H** White, Kelliher, D'Andrea	4:24 **P** Brenner (15) **B** Small **C** Thrasher **H** Sweeney, Ender, Taylor
4:32 **P** Higgins (15) **B** Novio **C** Kelliher **H** White, Tobin, D'Andrea	4:32 **P** Burlingame (15) **B** Nadeau **C** King **H** Sweeney, Taylor, Ender
4:40 **P** Brenner (15) **B** Kelliher **C** Tobin **H** Knox, Seguin, Scott	4:40 **P** Dillon (15) **B** Radulski **C** Ender **H** Delucia, Hartung, Slicer
4:48 **P** Burlingame (15) **B** Slicer **C** Kelliher **H** Delucia, Hartung, Scott, White	4:48 **P** Higgins (15) **B** Domenick **C** King **H** Knox, Sweeney, Seguin, Ender
4:56 **P** Dillon (15) **B** White **C** Delaney **H** Kelliher, Tobin, D'Andrea, Hewes	4:56 **P** Taylor (15) **B** Knox **C** Thrasher **H** Slicer, King, Rajotte, Duff
5:04 **P** Higgins (15) **B** Rajotte **C** Kelliher **H** Delucia, Scott, Hartung, White	5:04 **P** Burlingame (15) **B** Hewes **C** Ender **H** Knox, Seguin, Sweeney, Taylor
5:12 **P** Dryswak (15) **B** Seguin **C** Thrasher **H** Kelliher, Tobin, D'Andrea, King	5:12 **P** Beaudet (15) **B** Sweeney **C** Delaney **H** Ender, Taylor, Slicer, Ballard
5:20 **P** Burlingame (15) **B** Thrasher **C** King **H** Delucia, Hartung, Scott, White	5:20 **P** Higgins (15) **B** Delaney **C** Tobin **H** Knox, Sweeney, Seguin, Ender

Numbers in parentheses = number of pitchers; **P** = pitcher; **C** = catcher; **H** = hitter; **B** = charts pitches ment are placed at the top of the inning, followed by the number of pitches for that particular inning. Higgins and Burlingame throw 15 pitches the first inning. Brenner and Dillon throw 15 pitches the second inning. Burlingame and Higgins throw another 15 pitches the third inning. This continues until all pitchers have completed their long throwing. On this day, Higgins and Burlingame will throw 90 pitches over six innings.

The catcher (C) should be labeled under or next to the pitcher. During the first inning, Kelliher catches Higgins and Ender catches Burlingame. Underneath the catchers should be the hitters (H). In the first inning, Knox, Seguin, and Scott will hit against Higgins; Delucia, Hartung, and Slicer will hit against Burlingame. Each inning someone (B) is needed to chart the pitches thrown. Thomas and Dryswak will chart pitches the first inning.

PROVIDING LIVE PITCHING OPPORTUNITIES

A pitcher needs the chance to become both mentally and physically prepared for his game-day duties. As you well know, throwing to a batter in a game is completely different from throwing to a catcher in practice. By providing live pitching situations, you give your pitchers a chance to develop mechanics, endurance, and confidence in throwing strikes.

PITCHER DRILLS

Any team with visions of a championship season should have its pitchers spend time on all facets of the game, including fielding ground balls, covering bases, understanding plays, and becoming comfortable with the players behind them. We focus on pitcher drills four times a week, incorporating them into our practices Monday through Thursday.

In designing pitcher drills, try to provide as many repetitions for as many pitchers as possible as they learn to field bunts, cover bases, and hold runners. We strive for all pitchers, catchers, and infielders to become accustomed to working with each other. Each of the following pitcher drills may be used in limited space and can be completed in 15 to 20 minutes.

DRILL 1

FIELDING BUNTED BALLS

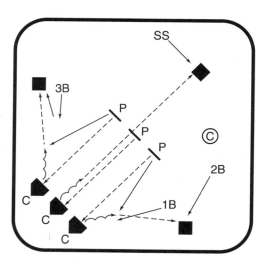

Goals. (1) To build communication skills between pitchers, catchers, and infielders. (2) To provide maximum repetitions in a limited amount of time.

Skills Emphasized:

- communication
- fielding
- throwing

Set-Up.   Fielding bunted balls incorporates all infielders, three catchers, and nine pitchers. Based on the size of the working area, a miniature infield needs to be constructed. There should be three catchers' plates at home, bases at first, second, and third, and three pitchers' plates about 8 to 10 ft apart and between 45 and 60 ft from the catchers. Three pitchers should be in line with each pitcher's plate.

Procedure.   The pitcher and catcher on the right side work with the first and second basemen. The pitcher and catcher in the middle work with the shortstop. The pitcher and catcher on the left side work with the third baseman.

Simultaneously, the three pitchers throw the ball to their respective catchers. Each catcher then rolls the ball as if the ball has been bunted. The catcher on the left rolls the ball toward third, the catcher on the right toward first, and the catcher in the middle back toward the middle pitcher. As the ball is being rolled, the right side catcher calls *one*. The pitcher and first baseman on the right side charge to field the bunted ball. The second baseman covers first. If the ball is rolled hard enough, the first baseman will call *me*, field the ball, and throw to the covering second baseman. If the ball is rolled softly, the first baseman will call *you*, and the pitcher will field the ball and throw to first, where either the first or second baseman will be covering.

In the middle, the catcher rolls the ball to the pitcher. As that catcher calls *two*, the pitcher fields the ball and throws to second base, where the shortstop is covering. The shortstop practices turning a double-play by flipping the ball to an extra player who is about 15 ft away toward first base.

On the left side, the catcher rolls the ball down the third base line and calls *three*. The pitcher and third baseman charge. The third baseman calls *you*. As the third baseman retreats and covers third, the pitcher fields the ball and makes a throw to third. After each ball is thrown to a base, the pitchers rotate to another line to practice each skill.

Coaching Points.   The focus of this drill is on communication. As the ball is rolled, the first baseman and the third baseman must call who will field the ball. The catcher must make a call as to where the ball will be thrown.

On the right side and in the middle, it is important for the player fielding the ball to set his feet toward and step in the direction of the base and to make an overhand throw to the base. On the left side, the pitcher must get to the baseline and, as he fields the ball, throw from the bent fielding position. This will save time in getting the ball to the base.

Variation.   If you have multiposition players or if you don't have enough pitchers to run this drill with three lines, you can easily do one section at a time. This will allow players to move into different positions.

Safety Concerns.   There will be three balls being thrown at once, so it is important that players know where to throw. Also, as the pitchers finish one station, they are to rotate around to another station. As they rotate, they need to be aware that other pitchers are still working and that balls will be thrown through certain lanes. If your gym or working area is not enclosed by netting, be certain that the area is clear. Also watch for stray balls caroming off walls.

DRILL

2

COVER FIRST, SQUEEZE, SQUEEZE

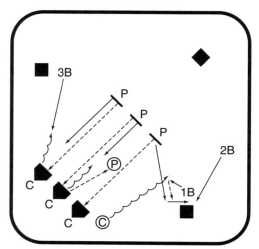

Goals. (1) To develop communication skills between all pitchers, catchers, and fielders. (2) To provide maximum repetitions in limited time and space. (3) To develop a unification between the pitchers and fielders

Skills Emphasized:

- communication
- fielding
- throwing

Set-Up. As in Drill 1, an infield must be constructed based on the size of the working area. You'll need three home plates and three pitcher's plates along with first and third base. Nine pitchers, three catchers, first, second, and third basemen, a coach or extra player to hit ground balls, and an extra fielder are needed to run this drill efficiently. If more infielders are available, they may form lines for rotation at first, second, and third base.

Procedure. On the right side of the infield, a pitcher, a catcher, the first and second basemen, and the extra player or coach work together on feeding repetitions to the pitcher covering first. In the middle, a pitcher, a catcher, and an extra player work on developing a squeeze double-play. On the left side, a pitcher, a catcher, and the third baseman work on the squeeze play.

Simultaneously, the three pitchers pitch the ball to their respective catchers. The coach on the right side hits the ball between the first and second basemen. Both the first and second basemen attempt to play the ball. Communication is vital. The player with the best chance of fielding the ball calls *me*, fields the ball, and makes a lead throw to the pitcher, who is now covering first.

In the middle group, the catcher rolls the ball back to the pitcher and calls *four*. The pitcher sprints off the mound, fields the ball, and makes an underhand flip to the catcher. The catcher stretches for the ball and practices turning a double-play with the extra fielder.

On the left side, the catcher rolls the ball down the third base line. Both the pitcher and third baseman charge. The third baseman calls either *me* or *you*. If the call is *me*, the third baseman fields the ball and makes an underhand flip to the catcher, who practices a tag on a close play at the plate. If the call is *you*, the pitcher fields the ball and makes an underhand flip to the catcher.

Coaching Points. The focus of the drill is on communication. The first, second, and third basemen must make a call regarding who should field the ball. For the catchers, it is necessary to call *four* on the squeeze plays.

As the pitcher on the right side covers first base, he should focus on finding the angle that puts him on the first base line about 15 to 20 ft from the bag. As he approaches first, he should stay to the inside of the foul line. After receiving the ball from either the first or second baseman, the pitcher should tag the inside of first base with his right foot and step beyond the bag with his left foot. He should then plant his right foot beyond the bag and turn to the infield, ready to make another play. Should the pitcher arrive at first base before the throw, he makes the play as though he is a first baseman.

In the middle and on the left side, the pitcher or the player making the suicide flip to the catcher must remember to keep himself low and allow his momentum to carry him to the catcher. Also, as the flip is being made, the tossing hand should stay *below* the waist to allow for a low, accurate flip.

Variation.   It is easy to take this drill one step further by adding the short-stop. In this variation, the pitcher covering first makes an extra throw to home and adds the shortstop to the left group in order to practice covering third.

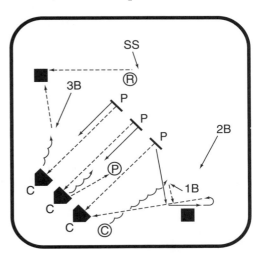

Simultaneously, all three pitchers pitch the ball to their respective catchers. As the right-side pitcher covers first and receives the ball from the first or second baseman, he crosses the inside of the bag, steps with his left foot, plants with his right foot, rotates, and throws home to his catcher.

On the left side of the infield, the shortstop covers third base. As the third baseman and the pitcher charge the ball, the catcher calls either *three* or *four* to simulate various game situations.

The group in the middle continues work on the squeeze double-play. The pitchers continuously rotate from line to line to get in as many repetitions as possible.

Safety Concerns.   Many balls are being thrown at once. Pitchers and players must keep themselves under control and be accurate with their throws. It is not important to throw the ball hard in this drill.

DRILL 3   *WILD PITCH*

Goals.   (1) To develop communication skills between the pitcher and catcher. (2) To develop ball-handling skills between the pitcher and catcher on wildly pitched balls.

Skills Emphasized:

- home plate coverage
- throwing

Set-Up.   Three catchers and nine pitchers are needed to run this drill. Three pitcher's plates are placed about 60 ft from home plate and about 15 to 20 ft from each other. There should be about 20 ft between home plate and the wall or netted area. If you are using a wall behind home plate, you should cover the wall with soft padding to create a dead effect. As the ball hits the wall or net, it should fall to the ground. It should not bounce back toward the catcher.

Procedure.   The three pitchers simultaneously throw their ball over the head and to the side of their catcher. As each catcher turns to retrieve the ball, each pitcher calls *left*, *middle*, or *right*, depending on where the catcher needs to go. Once the call is made, each pitcher sprints to cover home. The catcher retrieves the ball and makes an accurate throw to the pitcher.

Coaching Points.   Remember—the catcher is facing the pitcher, producing a mirror image, so the pitcher's call will be the *opposite* of what he sees. The pitcher's right is actually the catcher's left.

   As each pitcher covers home, he must keep his body open to the imaginary runner coming from third base. The pitcher should never turn his back to the runner while covering home plate. Right-handed pitchers will receive the ball from the catcher and make a tag straight down to the plate. Left-handed pitchers will make a sweep tag across the plate. Once the tag has been made, each pitcher must get out of the way of the slide.

Safety Concerns.   Any walls behind the catcher should be padded. An alternative is to use soft balls that won't bounce back off a wall.

DRILL

4

HOLDING RUNNERS

Goals.   (1) To develop communication and timing between the pitchers and all infielders. (2) To provide maximum repetitions in limited time.

Skills Emphasized:

- pitcher's pivots
- infielder's timely base coverage

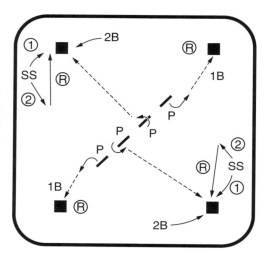

Set-Up.   This drill requires four to nine pitchers, two sets of middle infielders, and two first basemen. Extend four pitcher's plates to the middle of the working area and about 5 ft from each other. The two outside pitchers each work with a first baseman. The two inside pitchers each work with a pair of middle infielders. The sets of middle infielders are at opposite ends of the working area. Baserunners are needed at each base.

Procedure.   The two outside pitchers work with the first basemen to develop communication skills and to develop plays to hold the runner at first. As the pitchers come to the set position, they should concentrate on proper footwork as they throw to first. If the first baseman feels the runner is getting too big a lead or if he expects a bunt, he may use a break or two-step play.

   If the first baseman identifies a bunt situation, he may signal the break play. If the first baseman signals for the break play, the pitcher will come to the set position and, as the first baseman breaks toward home, deliver the ball to the catcher.

   In response to a bunt situation or a possible steal, the first baseman may also signal for the two-step play. If this occurs, the pitcher comes to the set position.

The first baseman takes two steps toward the plate, then stops and retreats to the bag. As he retreats to the bag, the pitcher turns and throws to first.

The middle pitchers work with the middle infielders on holding the runner at second base. As the pitcher comes to the set position, he gets a signal from the middle infielders. Right-handed pitchers get the signal from the shortstop, and lefties get the sign from the second baseman. Once the sign is received, the pitcher turns to the catcher, waits a predetermined time, then turns and throws to the appropriate player covering second. Pitchers should rotate to all four stations.

Coaching Points. Whenever a pitcher throws to a base, he points his stride foot and knee in the direction of the throw. He must also point his nonthrowing shoulder and elbow in the throwing direction.

Signs given to the pitcher from all infielders should be uniform throughout the team. Time allowed for the middle infielders to maneuver into position should be consistent.

Variation. If there are not enough players available, the drill may be cut in half, leaving one set of middle infielders and one first baseman to work with two lines of pitchers.

Safety Concerns. At first, this is a confusing drill. There will be four balls moving at the same time. All pitchers and infielders need to be aware of all throws. Again, pitchers should throw at only half- to three-quarter speed during this drill. Allow enough room to hold four pitching stations and to let the infielders maneuver. A regular size gym is adequate for this drill.

CHAPTER 5

Catchers

Catchers don't get thrown a lot of credit. They never get the win, even when they call a great game. They are seldom in the spotlight for their defense because they rarely get to make the great play. And they are constantly being run on— and often run *over*—by opposing baserunners, so their mistakes tend to be noticed more than the things they do well. But actually, catching is one of the most important positions in baseball. The catcher is the only position that the other seven fielders and the pitcher look at on each pitch. In a way, he is the coach on the field. He calls each pitch, sets the defense, and makes defensive calls on every batted ball, attempted bunt, attempted steal, and emerging rundown situation. Perhaps, out of all that his position requires, his most challenging duty is handling the pitching staff and getting the most out of the talent available.

Coach's Corner

Many catchers who have played for me have been drafted into professional baseball. Some have gone on to the next level because they are great throwers, others because they are great hitters. The one catcher whom I believed was the best of them all did not get drafted. He wasn't a great runner. He wasn't a great thrower. He wasn't even a good hitter. What he did well was something the scouts couldn't see: He knew how to handle a pitching staff.

UNDERSTANDING THE CATCHER'S ROLES

In developing catchers, it is important to understand their many roles. A catcher's first priority is to be a leader. He must be able to take charge of situations on the field. He must be able to make instant decisions yet have the strength to carry on when one of his decisions is wrong. He must be aggressively vocal and lead by example, but he cannot put himself above the players around him. He must be confident but not cocky.

A catcher's second priority is handling the pitching staff. This is a large chore because each pitching staff is made up of many pitchers. At Maine, each one of our catchers is responsible for knowing the ins and outs of all 16 pitchers on our staff each year. You may use just two catchers and eight pitchers, but each catcher has to be comfortable working with each pitcher if you are going to have a chance at success. The more experienced catchers should handle the more experienced pitchers and the catchers most likely to catch in games should handle top pitchers.

All successful teams have catchers who are confident in handling their pitchers. They have confidence in the decisions they make and in their ability to play the game. But ability alone doesn't make them the players they are. They must spend an endless amount of time developing, refining, and maintaining their skills. In handling a pitching staff, the catcher must

- be able to communicate with the pitcher,
- be able to get the borderline strikes through framing,
- know the strengths and weaknesses of each pitcher,
- know each pitcher's repertoire of pitches,
- know what each pitcher can throw for strikes, and
- know what the pitcher can throw for an out pitch.

The catcher's third priority is throwing. To be a *good* thrower, the catcher either has to have a great arm or be able to get rid of the ball quickly. To be a *great* thrower, he has to do both well. To contain good runners, the catcher must perfect his throwing techniques and accuracy through constant drilling. As you develop your daily, weekly, and seasonal practice plans for catchers, focus on four objectives:

- Developing a unison between the catchers and the pitching staff
- Developing receiving techniques
- Improving throwing techniques
- Gaining game experience

Developing catchers through game experience allows you to critique what the catcher is calling for a sequence of pitches. Is the catcher calling the right pitches to get ahead in the count? What is he calling when the pitcher is behind in the count? Is he getting the strike for the pitcher? If he is not meeting team needs at this point, it is a good time to develop the mental aspect of catching.

Establishing a set order for performing drills is the best way to develop your catchers. Breaking the program down into nine concentrated areas allows you to develop a catcher's throwing and fielding skills in a simplified manner.

THROWING DRILLS

We allot time in each practice—usually 30 minutes—for catcher drills. It's difficult to get our catchers together all at once (because they are catching pitchers), but there must be time allowed for them to get individual attention. Each catcher can do many of the following drills on his own.

DRILL

1 | GRIP

Goals. (1) To develop and increase the chance of finding the proper throwing grip. (2) To quicken the movement from ball in glove to throwing hand. (3) To consistently find the same throwing grip, with the index finger and middle finger across the wide horseshoe seams of the ball and the thumb tucked underneath.

Skills Emphasized:

- proper throwing grip
- proper hand movement

Set-Up. This drill can be done individually. The only equipment needed is a catcher's mitt and a ball.

Procedure. The catcher gets in his receiving position with a ball in his glove. His throwing hand should be behind his glove as though he is receiving a pitch. In one motion, he transfers the ball from his glove to his throwing hand. A catcher can complete 25 repetitions in a period of 4 or 5 minutes. The more repetitions completed, the better the catcher becomes at transferring.

Coaching Points. When players perform drills on their own, they have a tendency to get lazy or hurry through the drill. It is better to do 25 good repetitions than 50 hurried ones. Make sure the catcher takes his time. This is an important drill because it practices the beginning of the throwing process. If the catcher doesn't have a good grip, the throw has little chance of being a good one.

Variation. This drill is also good for catchers to do in pairs. They can coach each other through the drill and check that each is doing it correctly. Have one catcher be the receiver and the other the tosser. The two should be about 10 ft apart. The catcher is in his receiving position with glove hand extended and throwing hand behind the glove. The tosser flips the ball to the receiver. The receiver concentrates on receiving the ball and transferring it to the throwing hand. After 10 repetitions, the catchers change. Complete 3 sets of 10.

Safety Concerns. When doing catcher drills, your catcher should always wear a mask, chest protector, and shin pads. This will not only give protection but will get your catcher used to moving with the equipment on.

BOW AND ARROW

Goals. (1) To develop proper throwing grip. (2) To develop and decrease throwing release time.

Skills Emphasized:

- hand-eye coordination in receiving and throwing
- ball transfer from glove to throwing hand
- proper foot movement

Procedure. This is another drill that can be done individually. The first time through, the catcher needs only a ball. He should be facing a net or padded wall. In proper receiving position, with the ball in his throwing hand, he tosses the ball in the air. As it comes down, he steps to the ball and cradles it into his bare hand, framing it to get the strike. After framing, he transfers the ball to his throwing hand and sets himself to throw. When finished, he should have his hands in the bow and arrow position as he flips the ball into the net.

Coaching Points. This is a good drill for developing soft hands. It forces the catcher to pull the ball into his bare hand as he catches. As he becomes proficient at this, there will be less chance of him dropping balls.

No player should be standing around during practice. There is always some drill that he can do to better himself. This is a drill that can be performed every day. It is a good filler for when coaches are working with other players. All the catcher needs to do is grab a ball and go to work.

Variation. This same drill can be performed with a glove. With the glove on, a catcher must get used to transferring the ball to the bare hand. The drill is performed the same way as without the glove.

DRILL

3

SHOULDER TO NET

Goals. (1) To increase throwing strength. (2) To decrease ball transfer and release time. (3) To develop shoulder and hip rotation. (4) To develop a consistent release point.

Skills Emphasized:

- proper throwing grip
- proper footwork
- consistent throwing path

Procedure. This drill can be performed alone. The catcher stands with his glove hand and shoulder parallel to a net or padded wall. He should be 5 to 10 ft from the net. He tosses the ball into the air. Upon receiving it, he pulls the ball to the throwing position, rotates his upper body to the net, steps, and throws the ball into the net.

Coaching Points. The catcher does not need to throw hard. He is trying to develop quickness in releasing the ball and to develop a relationship between stepping and throwing to a target.

Variation. If time and space allow, place an infielder, preferably a shortstop or second baseman, at a base about 15 ft away. The catcher's glove hand and shoulder are parallel to the infielder. Again, he tosses the ball in the air, receives it, gets into throwing position, rotates his upper body, steps, and throws to the base.

Safety Concerns. Because of the short distance between the catcher and the fielder, the catcher should not throw hard. Remember, this drill is to develop quickness in release time.

DRILL 4   MOMENTUM

Goals.   (1) To develop strength in the throwing arm. (2) To decrease release time. (3) To increase throwing accuracy and gain momentum in the throwing direction.

Skills Emphasized:

- proper throwing arm path
- proper step and gained momentum toward target

Set-Up.   This drill involves four catchers. They stand in a square, perpendicular to one another and about 15 ft apart. One ball is used and the drill rotates clockwise.

Procedure.   As a catcher receives the ball, he quickly transfers the ball to the throwing hand, points the front shoulder, steps, and flips the ball to the next catcher. Beginning slowly and then increasing speed, the catchers continually move the ball.

Coaching Points.   During this drill, the catchers will tend to move too quickly too early. It is important that they begin slowly so they develop proper technique. As they get better, they may then increase their speed. This will force them to quicken their hand speed and coordinate their footwork.

Safety Concerns.   Catchers should be fully protected. At times, players rush, increasing the chance of a missed ball and possible injury.

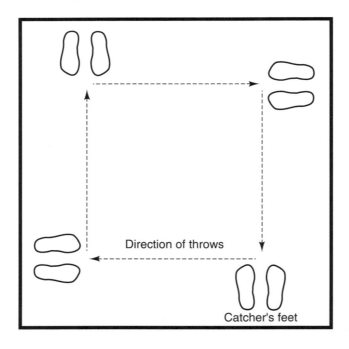

Direction of throws

Catcher's feet

DRILL 5 | LONG TOSS

Goals.   (1) To develop strength in the throwing arm. (2) To decrease release time. (3) To increase throwing accuracy.

Skills Emphasized:

- proper grip
- proper footwork
- proper throwing arm path

Set-Up.   This drill involves two or four catchers.

Procedure.   The throwing drill is broken down into two steps. In the first step, the catchers work individually. Each catcher has a ball, which he tosses in the air. As he catches the ball, he should work on getting the proper grip while taking the ball out of the glove as quickly as possible and getting it to throwing position with fingers on top of the ball. This step should be done 25 times daily.

In the second step, the catchers work in pairs about 70 ft apart. They need only one ball. As they throw the ball back and forth, they must work on the skills emphasized in the first step, developing proper grip while getting the ball to correct throwing position. As the catcher receives the ball, he should step with the appropriate foot and gain momentum in the direction of the throw.

Coaching Points.   The catchers need not throw hard. The emphasis is on developing proper footwork, gaining momentum, developing grips, and increasing accuracy and arm strength. As the preseason progresses, increase the distance between the catchers to develop arm strength.

Safety Concerns.   Catchers do as much throwing, if not more, than any player on the team. Monitor their throwing activities to ensure proper development and to decrease the chance of arm injuries.

RECEIVING DRILLS

Catchers proficient in framing pitches, throwing accurately, and controlling bad pitches are valuable to any team. The following drills will help your catchers learn these skills.

DRILL 6 — FRAMING

Goals.   (1) To develop the proper framing technique. (2) To develop soft hands.

Skills Emphasized:

- proper hand receiving angles
- learning to frame the right pitches
- learning to get the glove behind the ball

Set-Up.   This drill involves two or four catchers. Each should have a partner, preferably another catcher.

Procedure.   Each pair of catchers should be about 20 ft apart. Each group will need a ball and a home plate. One catcher assumes catching position behind home plate. The other catcher, playing pitcher, tosses the ball to the catcher. The catcher frames the pitch based on the location. After the first catcher has framed 25 pitches, the two switch places.

Coaching Points.   The catchers should frame only pitches that are strikes or borderline strikes. Any ball obviously out of the strike zone should not be framed. It is important that the catcher be able to keep the ball in the strike zone, even on borderline pitches. The receiving hand and arm should be relaxed. As the ball approaches the catcher, he rotates the hand to keep the ball over the plate.

Variation.   Catchers should work on framing the strike or near strike at every opportunity. This includes when they are catching pitchers who are stretch throwing, short throwing, or practicing live game situations. While loosening arms during warm-up is also a good opportunity for framing tossed balls.

Safety Concerns. Any time a catcher assumes the catching position, he should have a full set of gear on. This will make it easier for him to become accustomed to catching fully geared and will protect him from being hit and injured by poorly thrown balls.

FRAMING TO GRIP

Goals. (1) To combine framing skills and grip drills. (2) To quicken the movements from the receiving position to the grip position.

Skills Emphasized:

- proper receiving skills
- proper framing skills
- proper grip skills

Procedure. This drill is performed the same as Drill 6. Catchers work in pairs 20 ft apart. One catcher receives the other's tosses. The receiving catcher frames the ball and then transfers it from his glove to his throwing hand.

Safety Concerns. All catchers should wear full protective gear.

FRAMING TO THROWING

Goals.   (1) To develop framing, gripping, and throwing skills. (2) To quicken the throwing process.

Skills Emphasized:

- framing
- gripping
- throwing (positioning)

Procedure.   Again, catchers work in pairs 20 ft apart in full protective gear. One catcher receives the other's tosses. The catcher receiving the ball concentrates on framing, gripping, and getting the ball to throwing position.

Coaching Points.   Don't worry about your catchers' footwork yet. This will be developed in the next drill. During this drill, watch for your catchers getting the ball from the glove hand to the throwing hand and then to the upper body and throwing position. Use the bow and arrow technique where the lead elbow extends to the designated position and the throwing hand goes straight to the ear with elbow extended.

Safety Concerns.   Each catcher should be fully geared.

DRILL 9

STEPPING TO THROWING

Goals. (1) To increase throwing quickness. (2) To increase throwing angles. (3) To decrease throwing distance. (4) To develop timing.

Skills Emphasized:

- proper read angles
- proper footwork

Set-Up. Catchers work in groups of two, with a ball and a home plate for each group.

Procedure. Each set of catchers positions about 30 ft apart. One catcher assumes the catching position. His partner throws the ball toward the plate. The catcher steps to the ball with the appropriate foot, gets his body in front of the ball, receives the ball, and moves to throwing position. After 25 repetitions, the players switch.

Coaching Points. The tossers should vary the location of the throws. This forces the receiving catcher to read the angle of the throw and make a habit of using proper footwork.

Variation. Any time a catcher is playing pass or long tossing, he should work on stepping to the ball. This will force him to get his body in front of the ball and will help him gain momentum in the throwing direction.

DRILL

10 | BLOCKING OR BAD BALL

Goals. (1) To learn to read the spin and bounce of poorly thrown balls. (2) To develop proper footwork in moving to block bad balls. (3) To learn to get behind the ball.

Skills Emphasized:

- increase lateral movement
- proper drop techniques
- proper blocking angles

Set-Up. Catchers work in pairs. Each pair needs one complete set of catching gear, a home plate, and five baseballs.

Procedure. One catcher is fully geared and in catching position behind home plate. The other catcher is the thrower. He positions about 30 ft from the catcher. The thrower tosses the ball so that it bounces about 2 ft in front of the catcher. The catcher works on reading the ball's spin, moving in the direction of the throw, getting behind the ball, and blocking the ball with his chest, arms, legs, and glove.

Coaching Points. The catcher must do whatever he can to save the pitch. When possible, he should step with the foot facing the direction of the ball and drop the inside knee to the ground. As he blocks the ball, he should angle his body and open and flatten his glove to deflect the ball toward the plate. After 25 repetitions, the players switch.

Variation. If you don't have enough catching gear for all the groups, use tennis balls instead of baseballs. Whether they are catching in the bullpen, warming up pitchers, short throwing, or long throwing, catchers should always work on blocking pitches.

Safety Concerns. Catchers should be geared at all times. Even if you are using tennis balls, the catcher should wear a mask to protect his face.

DRILL 11   COMBINATION

Goals. (1) To practice Drills 1 through 10. (2) To increase throwing strength. (3) To quicken release time. (4) To develop and quicken footwork. (5) To coordinate base coverage between fielders and catchers. (6) To gain momentum in the throwing direction.

Skills Emphasized:

- proper framing technique
- proper footwork, grip, and release point

Set-Up. If possible, place home plate and second base 124 ft apart. The catcher assumes position behind the plate, ready to receive. A shortstop and second baseman take their positions. If space allows, they should be about 15 ft from the base. A pitcher should be 60 ft, 6 in. from the catcher and aligned directly between the plate and second base. Place a hitter on either side of the plate.

Procedure. The pitcher works from the set position. After receiving the sign from the catcher, he delivers the ball to the plate. The catcher frames the ball and then throws to second base, where the shortstop or second baseman is covering.

Coaching Points. To give the catcher different looks, move the hitters to different positions in the batter's box and switch hitters to different sides of the plate. Rotate the catchers every three or four throws. Rotate the pitchers and fielders so that all players involved get used to playing with each other.

Variations. If you have more than one catcher and set of infielders and space allows, set up two or even three stations.

This drill can be done at third base, using the same format as just described. Home plate and third base should be 90 ft apart. The mound should be 60 ft, 6 in. from both bases and at the correct angle. The pitcher, catcher, third baseman, and hitter assume their positions. The pitcher receives the sign and delivers the ball to the plate. The catcher frames the pitch and throws to third, where the third baseman is covering.

Rotate all players at all positions so that they become used to one another. If space is available, set up more than one drill.

Safety Concerns. In this drill, communication is essential for safety. The middle infielder must communicate who is covering the base. The pitcher needs to be conscious of the catcher's throw.

CHAPTER 6

Infielders

Executing and practicing all ball-handling drills daily is critical in a player's developing and mastering the basic skills he needs to be a successful infielder and a contributor to a top defensive team.

All infielders must get repetitions each day to develop properly. This means drilling players on the fundamentals until they receive enough repetitions to become adept at fielding and throwing. Once the skills have been developed, infielders must practice to maintain those skills.

Fashion drills that call for execution of the basic infield techniques as the player fields, handles, and throws the ball. Drills also need to be developed that help the infielder master the timing and execution of all multiplayer ball-handling situations, with an emphasis on all double-play possibilities.

If you're practicing indoors where time and space are limited, you need to prioritize all infield drillwork based on your philosophy of infield play and defense. We believe basic fielding skills and the ability to turn the double-play are critical in developing good defensive teams. Your team's ability to consistently make the routine play will help you prevent the opponent's big innings. Being able to consistently turn the double-play will put you on track to being a championship team.

As you plan your infield practice drills, gear them to

- developing timing between players,
- developing execution of infield fundamentals,
- developing execution of proper throwing accuracy,
- developing lateral movement, and
- developing daily double-play, ball-handling routines.

DEVELOPING TIMING

Knowing where your teammates are and where they are going to be in all situations increases your chances of making defensive plays. Being in the right cut position, knowing where to go to back up a base, and understanding your teammates' abilities play an important role in a team's success.

When your season begins, you must believe in your team's ability to handle all situations, including basic plays, double-plays, cuts, relays, team positioning, and continuity. You must be confident that each player knows the game and his role as part of the defensive unit.

Each athlete also must have confidence in himself and his teammates. Through drills and the time you spend on situations, your players will know what to do on the field. They will know where their teammates will be in all situations. They will know that someone will be there to back up or help out if needed. By developing these attitudes, your players will be more aggressive and confident in attacking the ball.

EXECUTING INFIELD FUNDAMENTALS

Teams that cannot make the routine play are going to struggle, no matter how good the pitching is. Basic skill drills must be performed every day. If time is limited, use a drill that allows your players the most repetitions. The square drill (Number 4 on page 68) is ideal for this. You may have other ideas, but repetitions are a must.

Coach's Corner

I remember Mike Bordick once said, "A pitcher's best friend is his infield." I agree with Mike. I have never known a pitcher who can control a whole game. No pitcher strikes out 27 batters every time out—consequently, fielding skills are a must. In 1982 for example, we were squared off against Cal-State Fullerton at the College World Series. Joe Johnson (Atlanta Braves) was pitching a masterful game and finished with a complete game shut-out. As Joe will tell you to this day, his infield saved him. Jeff Paul (Texas Rangers), Pete Adams (New York Yankees), Mark Sutton (Texas Rangers), and Kevin Bernier turned four double-plays during the game. Without the double-plays, we probably would have lost.

PERFECTING THROWING ACCURACY

Throwing requires great concentration on the part of the fielder. Many errors are caused by hurried throws or careless attempts at throwing. To minimize the chance of throwing errors, incorporate drills into your routine that cut down on the distance that infielders have to throw to certain bases. You are trying to make them more aggressive in attacking the ball and helping them gain momentum toward the throwing target.

In any drill you use, make infielders aware of cutting distances. Constantly strive and push them to be aggressive. This will not only cut down on the distance of the throws, it will give your fielders confidence in their abilities.

DEVELOPING LATERAL MOVEMENT

Quickness is critical in covering ground, but many infielders have such poor first-step movement that time and distance are wasted. As you and the players work drill after drill, concentrate on developing first-step quickness. This will allow your fielders to cover more ground and take away some would-be hits.

PRACTICING DOUBLE-PLAYS

Infield drills have many purposes, the most important being to improve ball handling between players. Once players are accustomed to each other's timing, the chance for error decreases and the chance for success increases. As you develop practice sessions, make sure you involve the utility infielders. The player who is most likely to fill in must get used to playing with the starters. It is necessary to rotate the utility infielder in to the position he will play.

Coach's Corner

I remember a season that we did not turn a double-play for the first five games. We had plenty of chances but something always got in the way—a throwing error, a fielding error, or just lack of speed at making the turn. We lost four of those five games. Finally, we started to click. The fielders became used to each other and gained confidence in themselves and their teammates' abilities. We went on to be a regional team, finished with 40+ wins, and became adept at turning the double-play. Three of those four infielders went on to be drafted.

INDIVIDUAL DRILLS

DRILL 1 *THROWING WARM-UP DRILL*

Goals. (1) To slowly warm up the muscles of the body and the throwing arm. (2) To develop the proper throwing grip.

Skills Emphasized:

- proper throwing technique
- proper arm path

Procedure. Each infielder should have a partner directly across from him about 10 to 15 ft away. With bodies squared and feet together, the infielders throw the ball back and forth.

Coaching Points. The infielder should not step as he throws. His feet are to stay together. The fielder should use the four-seam grip. Like a pitcher, he should pull the ball down and out of the glove, point the front shoulder and elbow toward the target, and spin the ball to his partner. He should finish with his armpit over the opposite knee and elbow by the knee.

Safety Concerns.   This drill is strictly a warm-up drill to loosen the arm and practice proper throwing form. The fielders should throw with ease, spinning the ball to their partners.

DRILL 2   ONE-KNEE WARM-UP

Goals.   (1) To develop a perfect stride location in which the knee and toe point in the direction of the desired target. (2) To establish a correct and consistent path of the arm. (3) To ensure the proper follow-through.

Skills Emphasized:

- throwing
- concentration

Procedure.   This is the same as Step 2 in the 6-step warm-up (see the One-Knee drill, page 26). Two infielders square and position about 20 ft apart. Both fielders kneel on the push-off leg with the stride leg bent and pointed toward

the desired target. With the ball in his throwing hand, the thrower rotates his upper body so the nonthrowing shoulder and elbow point to the target as he raises his arm into cocked position. He focuses on the target, transfers his weight from back leg to front leg, and uncoils his upper body to allow for the explosion and the travel of the arm, elbow, shoulder, and hip. The two infielders continue until they are loose.

Coaching Points.   The four-seam grip should be used to keep the ball from tailing. Middle infielders should work together. First and third basemen should work together. Catchers should work together.

DRILL

3 ONE-ON-ONE FIELDING

Goal. To develop ground ball fielding skills through maximum repetitions in limited time.

Skills Emphasized:

- basic footwork
- fielding
- lateral movement
- gained momentum

Set-Up. A regular-sized gym will allow for 10 infielders and outfielders to work at once. Line half of the infielders down the middle of the gym. They will be the fielders and should be about 5 to 7 ft apart. Each fielder must have a partner, who faces him about 10 ft away. The partners are the rollers. Each set of partners needs a ball.

Procedure. Tell everyone which way to roll the ball. When you blow a whistle or call *roll*, rollers roll the ball in the direction of the call. The fielders shuffle to the ball, field it, and work on gaining momentum toward the throwing target. After fielding the ball, the fielder flips the ball back to the roller and returns to the original position to begin again. After a designated number of repetitions, the fielders and rollers switch positions.

Coaching Points. This drill is fantastic for teaching the fundamentals of fielding. It is important for the fielders to keep their rear-ends low and field the ball out in front of them with two hands. As infielders feather the ball to the belly, they must shuffle their feet and gain momentum in the throwing direction. While shuffling their feet and gaining momentum, the fielders should develop the proper grip and point the front shoulder in the throwing direction.

Variations. One-on-one fielding drills can be done bare-handed, using soft-hand equipment, or using a glove. All three methods are beneficial. Soft hands are stiff, flat, glove-sized surfaces that fit over and replace the glove as teaching tools in fielding ground balls and in turning double-plays. One-on-one fielding drills can be performed by two players. This is a good drill for coaches to have ready for those players with idle time.

Safety Concerns. You should tell the players which direction to roll the ball. This will keep your fielders from colliding. The fielders are not to throw the ball. After fielding it, they merely flip the ball back to their partner.

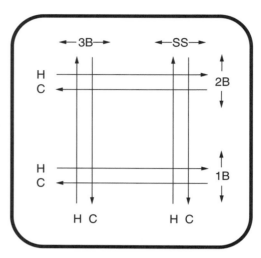

DRILL
4   *SQUARE DRILL*

Goals.   (1) To serve as the key drill in developing execution of fielding balls hit directly at, to the left, and to the right of the fielder. (2) To develop proper grip of the ball. (3) To develop proper footwork in gaining momentum in the direction of the throw. (4) To involve all infielders and outfielders.

Skills Emphasized:

- footwork
- fielding
- throwing

Set-Up.   The square drill is the best drill for developing infielders, as it gives each fielder many repetitions in a short time. An open area the size of a basketball court is most beneficial. Four coaches or players are needed to hit ground balls, and four others are needed to receive throws from the fielders. Four to 12 players are needed to field ground balls.

The fielders are set in their normal positions around the infield. Reserves and outfielders fill in behind the infielders, placing three players at each fielding position. You need to have one hitter and one receiver opposite each fielding position. Once all fielders, hitters, and receivers are in position, the configuration will look like a square.

Procedure.   Each hitter hits a ground ball to his respective fielder. Once the fielder has received the ground ball, he throws to his respective catcher. After the fielder finishes taking a ground ball, he goes to the end of the line until his turn comes again. Players continually rotate in their respective lines.

Coaching Points.   This drill takes about 15 minutes (5 minutes per fielding angle). The first 5 minutes are designated for ground balls hit directly at the fielders. The next 10 minutes are for fielders to work on lateral movement (fielding ground balls to their left and to their right).

As players perform the drill, they need to concentrate on developing the ability to field the ball, find the proper throwing grip, gain momentum in the throwing direction, institute a crow hop, point the front shoulder in the throwing direction, and develop a strong, overhand throw. Players must develop and execute movement and momentum to the ball and in the throwing direction to decrease the throwing distance.

Variation.   If space is limited, it is possible to perform the drill with two lines instead of one. The only drawback is the limited number of repetitions a player will receive.

Safety Concerns.   Communication between you and your players is crucial. As players move to the left and the right, they all should go in the same direction. This will keep players from colliding. Because there are four balls in play at all times, let stray balls that roll toward the middle of the fielding area go until the drill is completed. This will keep players from being hit.

TEAM AND POSITION DRILLS

DRILL 5

MULTIPLE BALL HANDLING

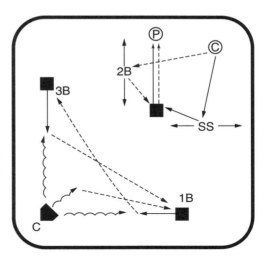

Goals. (1) To develop timing between fielders. (2) To develop proper techniques in turning the double-play. (3) To develop communication between fielders.

Skills Emphasized:

- footwork
- ball handling
- feeds

Set-Up. An area the size of a basketball court is needed to run this drill. In one designated area, the middle infielders, one first baseman, and a coach will work together on turning double-plays. In another designated area, the catchers, third basemen, the rest of the first basemen, and one coach will work together on slow rolling or dead ground balls. There should be at least two players at each position. The working area will be split in half. Both groups of fielders will be working simultaneously. Allow about 10 to 15 minutes for work on this drill.

Procedure: Shortstops, Second Basemen, First Basemen. In the double-play area with the middle infielders, time should be allotted for 6-4-3 and 4-6-3 double-play balls hit directly at, to the left, and to the right of the shortstop and the second baseman. Spend 5 minutes a day on each angle. In this short amount of time, each set of middle infielders will turn about 100 double-plays. The shortstops and second basemen will be at their respective positions and at double-play depth. The first baseman will be about 50 ft from second base ready to receive throws from the shortstops and second basemen. Toward home plate, a coach will be about 50 ft from second base. He will hit or roll ground balls to the middle infielders. Forty to fifty baseballs are needed to give maximum repetitions in a minimum amount of time.

For the first 5 minutes, hit or roll ground balls directly at the middle infielders, first hitting a bucket of balls to the shortstops and then a bucket to the second basemen. Devote the second 5 minutes to fielding ground balls to the inside toward second base of the middle infielders, with one bucket of balls being hit to the shortstops and one bucket being hit to the second basemen. Allot the last 5 minutes for fielding ground balls to the infielders away from second base. Each time a ball is hit, the fielding infielder will feed a double-play throw to his partner. The infielder turning the double-play will make a strong, overhand throw to the awaiting first baseman. As the first baseman receives the throw, he places the balls in a bucket to his left. Once the coach has completed hitting a bucket of balls, the first baseman runs his bucket to the coach and takes the empty bucket back to first.

Procedure: Catchers, Third Basemen, First Basemen. You will work with your players in the slow roller, dead ball, squeeze area. The first and third basemen will be at their respective positions about 70 ft from the catcher. You will be about 5 ft behind the catcher. Devote 5 minutes to each fielding section, slow rollers, dead ball, and squeeze plays. You will need six balls for these drills.

In the slow roller or moving-ball drill, slowly roll the ball toward the mound. The catcher fields the ball and makes an overhand throw to first. Next, slowly roll a ball down the third base line. The third baseman fields the ball and throws to first. Then slowly roll the ball down the first base line. The first baseman fields the ball and throws to third. The players continually rotate within their positions.

The dead-ball drill is similar to the slow roller, but the ball isn't moving. Place a ball about 5 ft in front of home plate. The catcher fields the ball and throws overhand to first. The first baseman flips the ball to the catcher, who places it about 10 ft in front of first base. The first baseman fields the ball and makes a strong overhand throw to third. The third baseman fields the ball and flips it to a catcher who is about 10 ft in front of third. Have the catcher place the ball on the ground. Have the third baseman field the ball and throw to first. The players rotate within their positions and the cycle begins again.

Devote the last 5 minutes to the squeeze play. With the same format of the last two drills, roll the ball down the third base line. The third baseman calls, fields the ball, and flips it underhand to the catcher covering home plate. As the third baseman flips the ball to the catcher, the catcher steps to the ball with his left foot to force the runner at home, pivots, and makes a strong overhand throw to first base to complete the double-play.

The second part of the squeeze play drill involves the catcher practicing the sweep tag. Roll the ball down the first base line. Have the first baseman call for the ball, field it, and flip it underhand to the catcher. The catcher receives the ball and makes a sweep tag at home plate. The players continually rotate within their positions, and the cycle begins again.

Coaching Points: Shortstops, Second Basemen, First Basemen.   There are many general points of emphasis in coaching the double-play. The feeding infielder is responsible for fielding the ball and feeding it in as little time as possible to a location demanded by the receiving infielder. All fielding and throwing actions are designed to make an easy and visible feed to the receiving infielder. The receiving fielder must get to the bag under control and demand a location for the feeding infielder to throw the ball. The receiving infielder must execute his footwork at the bag in a way that permits him to gain maximum momentum toward first base when turning the double-play. As the receiving infielder gathers the ball, he merely redirects the ball toward first base. While redirecting the ball, the receiving infielder must get the appropriate grip and make an effective, quick, and strong throw to first base. The receiving infielder should take care not to cup the ball (wrap his glove around the ball and throwing hand—this wastes valuable time in getting the ball out of the glove and to the first baseman).

While there are many general points of emphasis in turning the double-play, it is important to understand the individual coaching points of each middle infield position as the players field the ball from different angles and feed the ball to the covering infielder.

There are general guidelines the second baseman and shortstop must follow in fielding and feeding the ball on double-play attempts. The shortstop and second baseman must think about getting two outs on all balls hit directly to them and on all balls hit toward the middle of the infield and to the bag.

On a ball hit straight at him, the second baseman must stay low with hands extended as he fields the ball. Upon feathering the ball to his body, he swings from facing the ball to a position that faces directly toward the receiving shortstop by turning his hips and dropping his back foot so his belly button faces second base. With his belly button facing the shortstop, the second baseman flips overhand directly to the shortstop's desired receiving target.

On balls hit directly at him, the shortstop fields the ball squarely. Once he has done so, he clears his body and glove so the second baseman can see the ball. The shortstop then makes a direct throw to the second baseman's desired receiving target.

On balls hit to the middle of the diamond or toward second base, momentum is the key for middle infielders turning a double-play. On balls fielded by the second baseman to his right or toward the bag, he must keep his momentum going toward second as he fields the ball. He must make an underhand or backhand flip to the covering shortstop. As the second baseman flips the ball, his hand should not go any higher than his stomach. This will keep the ball from sailing. After he has flipped the ball, his momentum should continue toward the desired target to assure proper flight.

As the shortstop fields a ground ball to his left or toward the bag, he must keep his momentum going toward the bag. While moving to the ball, he must pivot off his left foot and step with his right foot toward the receiving person. To save time, the shortstop should not bring the ball behind the right leg in a bowling action. He should directly flip the ball from his glove. As he makes the flip, his momentum should carry toward second base.

On all balls hit away from the bag, the middle infielders must get at least one out. Getting two outs makes for an outstanding play. On balls hit away from the bag, the receiving fielder becomes a first baseman—that is, he goes for the ball and makes certain he gets an out.

On balls hit to his left, the second baseman must field the ball off the left foot, step and plant with the right foot, pivot, and throw overhand toward second base. Balls hit to the shortstop's right or toward third can be fielded two ways. If possible, the shortstop surrounds the ball, stops, bends off the back knee, faces second base, and throws overhand directly at the desired target. Most of the time, the shortstop will backhand the ball off the left foot, stop momentum off the right foot, pivot, and throw overhand toward the desired target.

Coaching Points: Catchers, Third Basemen, First Basemen. Slow rollers hit to the third baseman must be fielded off the left foot. As his momentum carries him through the ball, the third baseman flips the ball to first. Left-handed first basemen handle the slow roller the same way as the third baseman. With his momentum carrying him through the ball, the left-handed first baseman fields the ball off the right foot and flips it to third. A right-handed first baseman must swing his right foot over the slow-rolling ball, field the ball in the middle of his body, pivot, and make a strong overhand throw to third base. The emphasis to fielding a slow-rolling grounder is to keep the body's momentum going through the ball toward home and fielding the ball with the glove.

Catchers fielding slow-rolling grounders attack and field the ball differently on balls down the first and third base lines than they do on balls hit back toward the mound. On balls hit down the third base line, the catcher fields the ball facing the line. Upon feathering the ball to the belly and throwing position, he turns the glove sideways, steps toward first, and makes a strong overhand throw to first. On balls bunted toward the mound, the catcher surrounds the ball, rotates the glove shoulder toward first, and makes a strong overhand throw to first. Balls hit to the first base side will have the catcher fielding the ball square to the line. As he gathers the ball to throwing position, he drops his back foot away from the baseline (clearing the throw from hitting the runner), steps, and makes a strong overhand throw to first.

In fielding dead balls, the emphasis is again on keeping the body's momentum going through the ball. As the fielder attacks the ball, he reaches for it from the top down to get the right grip. This is not a scoop motion but a *drive* motion. As the fielder drives down and fields the ball bare-handed, he throws directly to the appropriate base. There is no need for the fielder to push the ball back into the glove, as this wastes time getting rid of the ball.

In fielding the squeeze, emphasis is again on the first and third basemen keeping their momentum going through the ball. As they field the ball, they must flip underhand to the catcher. As the flip is being made, the flip hand should not rise higher than the waist. Remember—on squeeze bunts fielded by the third baseman, the catcher executes a 5-2-3 double-play. On squeeze bunts fielded by the first baseman, the catcher executes a sweep tag.

In both drills, the middle infielders, corner players, and catchers work at the same time. While the middle infielders work on balls hit directly at them, the catchers and corner players work on slow rollers. Next, the middle infielders work on fielding balls hit to the bag while catchers and corner players work on fielding dead balls. Finally, the middle infielders work on fielding balls hit away from the bag while catchers and corner players work on fielding squeeze bunts. Each session should last about 5 minutes, with the total session lasting about 15 minutes.

Variation.   Due to limited space, some programs may have to develop multiple ball drills separately. This can be done, but it will take twice as much time. Middle infielders may use soft-hand equipment to teach them to redirect the ball.

Safety Concerns.   Groups will be working near each other. Players must take care not to run into each other or make errant throws. This drill is not designed as a speed contest. Players should be concerned with proper fielding and throwing techniques. Also, throws may skip away from fielders. Players must pay attention at all times, and communication is critical. Each player must know who he is working with.

DRILL
6

5-4-3; 3-6-3

Goals.   (1) To maximize use of time and space while developing ball-handling skills between infield double-play combinations. (2) To develop unison in double-play combinations between the first baseman and shortstop and between the third baseman and the second baseman.

Skills Emphasized:

- fielding
- throwing
- footwork

Set-Up.   Divide into two groups: third, second, and first basemen for the 5-4-3 drill and first basemen and shortstops for the 3-6-3 drill. To run these drills, you need a regular-size gym, all your infielders, two hitters, and two catchers. The third basemen, second basemen, and one of the first basemen position about 70 ft from each other in their infield positions. The second first baseman and the shortstop are about 70 ft from each other. One hitter and one catcher are on the first base side, facing the third baseman. Another hitter and catcher are on the third base side, facing the second group of first basemen.

Procedure. Hitter 1 hits a ground ball to the third baseman, who fields the ball, steps, and throws to the second baseman. The second baseman pivots, redirects the ball, and throws to first, completing a 5-4-3 double-play. The first baseman flips the ball to the catcher, and the cycle continues again.

In the meantime, the hitter facing the first basemen hits a ground ball to the first baseman. The first baseman fields the ground ball, pivots, steps, and throws overhand to the shortstop covering second base. The shortstop receives the ball, redirects it, and makes a strong overhand throw back to the first baseman, completing a 3-6-3 double-play. The first baseman flips the ball to the catcher, and the cycle continues. For all players to get an equal amount of work, all infielders should rotate within their positions. This will continue as the first and third basemen field ground balls hit directly at them, to their left, and to their right.

Coaching Points. The 3-6-3 double-play has three points of emphasis. When a left-handed first baseman fields a ball, he should receive the ball squarely. Then he should point his glove-side shoulder and elbow toward second base, step, and make a strong overhand throw to second. After throwing, he should look over his inside shoulder, find first base, return to the bag, and stretch for the return throw from the shortstop.

Ground balls hit to a right-handed infielder will be fielded differently. On a ball hit directly at him, a right-handed first baseman will field the ball squarely. He should then hop and spin toward second by swinging his right leg 180 degrees so that his left shoulder is pointing toward the bag. After making a strong overhand throw to second, the first baseman should find first base by looking over his inside shoulder, return to the bag, and stretch for the return throw from the shortstop. Balls hit to his left or down the line require the first baseman to field the ball, turn, swing glove side, step, and make a strong overhand throw to second. Again, he looks over his inside shoulder, finds the bag, and returns to take a throw from the shortstop. Ground balls hit to his right should be fielded squarely if possible. If not, he must backhand the ball, swing his back leg, point his front shoulder, and make a strong overhand throw to second base. Again, he looks over his inside shoulder, finds first, and returns to the bag to take a throw from the second baseman.

Communication is crucial in turning the 3-6-3 double-play. As the first baseman fields the ball, it is critical that the shortstop make an inside or outside call, depending on where the ball is fielded. If the first baseman fields the ball on the infield side of the baserunner, the shortstop calls inside and demands the ball on the inside. If the first baseman fields the ball on the outfield side of the baserunner, the shortstop calls outside and demands the ball on the outside of the bag.

In turning the 5-4-3 double-play, all balls hit directly at or to the left of the third baseman should be a double-play. As the third baseman fields the ball, he steps directly at second base and makes a strong overhand throw to the second baseman's point of demand. On balls hit to his right, the third baseman should surround the ball if possible. If surrounding the ball is not possible, the third baseman must backhand the ball on the left foot, step and arrest momentum on the right foot, point the glove shoulder toward second, and make a strong overhand throw to the second baseman's demand point. The second baseman must step to the ball to guarantee at least one out. In executing the double-play, nothing changes for the second baseman.

Spending 10 minutes on this drill will give your infielders enough repetitions at all angles. Spend the first 5 minutes on balls hit directly at and to the outfield side of the first basemen turning the 3-6-3 double-play. At the same time, the third basemen will field balls directly at and to the left in turning the 5-4-3 double-play. The next 5 minutes is spent as the first basemen field balls on the infield side of the baserunner and the third basemen field the ball hit down the line.

Variations. Due to space requirements and the number of people involved, this drill can be split into two sections, the first drill involving the 5-4-3 double-play and the second involving the 3-6-3. Soft-hand equipment may be used by the shortstop and second baseman to replace the glove.

Safety Concerns. Align both sets of bases in a way that is safe for all involved. After the 5-4-3 double-play drill has been set, offset and angle the 3-6-3 double-play drill to make the first baseman and shortstop safe from errant throws.

CHAPTER 7

Outfielders

All outfielders do not have the speed of Kenny Lofton, the arm of Mark Whiten, or the athletic ability of Bobby Kelly. These men have special, raw talents that can't be taught. Yet they did not become major league superstars on ability alone. They have spent many long, grueling hours developing their talents.

Developing outfielders requires the same goal-setting as any other position. You need to prioritize your objectives and formulate practice sessions that give your outfielders the quality repetitions they need for proper development. Whether you're practicing indoors or out, your outfielders need work on the basic fundamentals: communication, getting good jumps, fielding, catching, and throwing. The space available to you will dictate how you develop practice but should not limit you in any drills except fly balls. The drills at the end of this chapter can all be performed indoors as well as out.

COMMUNICATION

It is important to develop your players' verbal skills as well as their physical skills. Most important to developing outfielders is instituting a communication system. Good communication between outfielders both increases their chances of making the play and reduces the chances of their colliding and seriously hurting themselves.

The center fielder has priority calls over the other outfielders. He is the leader of the outfielders, and any ball he can get to is his. Your practices should include situations that force the outfielders to communicate with one another and enable the center fielder and his teammates to become comfortable with his taking charge.

BUILDING ARM STRENGTH

Building arm strength takes time. The outfielder's arm usually takes about 4 weeks to gain full strength. The key in developing good throwers is to throw often. Throwing every other day strengthens the arm and develops arm speed.

The one drill we use every other day is the long toss (explained in the drill section). As the season nears, our outfielders throw 5 out of 7 days.

ANGLE, JUMPS, AND FIELDING

Making good reads of balls coming off the bat and taking proper drop steps is essential in covering more ground, taking away would-be hits, and cutting off potential extra-base hits. The first step to teach is the ready position that allows your outfielder to move in any direction at a moment's notice. On balls hit at an angle, the outfielder needs to step with the outside foot at an angle that takes him to the spot where the ball will land. For example, if the ball is hit to the right of the fielder, he steps with his right foot first. On balls hit directly at him, the fielder takes his first step with his glove-side foot (right-handed throwers will start with their left foot).

After catching the ball, the outfielder must stop his momentum on his throwing foot and set to throw the ball back into the infield. Coordinating footwork, reading proper angles, and positioning to get the ball back to the infield quickly are essential to the outfielder's success.

OUTFIELD DRILLS

We incorporate outfield drills into practice 4 days a week. This allows ample time to develop the skills necessary for our outfielders to be successful. We practice communication and throwing drills 4 days per week and angle, jump, and fielding drills 3 days per week. How you incorporate the drills into your practice depends on your facilities. We play indoor intersquad games 3 days a week, which leaves us the other 4 days for drillwork. Your facilities may force you to design practice differently. If you are unable to play practice games, you can spend more days working on drills.

Outfielders must practice every day. If you are practicing inside, the outfielders will have the biggest adjustment when the team gets outside because they have not seen the ball come off the bat at short, long, quick, and sharp slicing angles. If your outfielders have developed the basic fundamentals, it will be quicker and easier for them to adjust to the flight and the appropriate angles of the ball coming off the bat.

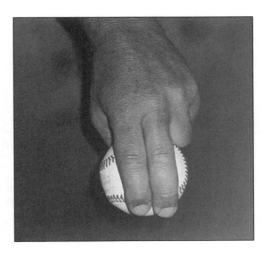

DRILL

1 | *ONE-KNEE THROWING*

Goals. (1) To develop proper throwing techniques. (2) To build arm strength. (3) To develop a quick release.

Skill Emphasized:

* throwing (proper grip, arm path, and throwing action)

Procedure. This is the same drill the pitchers use in the 6-step routine. Outfielders work in pairs about 15 ft apart and squared to each other. They throw the ball back and forth, concentrating on proper throwing techniques.

Coaching Points. A proper grip on the ball is essential. The outfielder should use a four-seam grip, with pointer and middle finger over the fat, horseshoe seams of the ball. The thumb is tucked underneath, opposite the top fingers. This grip will keep the ball from tailing on the throw. As the outfielder prepares to throw the ball, he should point his front shoulder and elbow toward the desired target, keep the throwing elbow at shoulder height, and exaggerate reaching for the sky. After releasing the ball, the outfielder should concentrate on sweeping the armpit over the knee, and the elbow by the knee.

Safety Concerns. This drill develops arm strength and helps the arm stretch out. To develop their arms, outfielders need to throw almost every day. If they do not adequately stretch and properly throw, the throwing arm and shoulder will tire and become sore. If this occurs, the player needs to take a day or two off, which puts him behind schedule in development.

DRILL 2   *90 DEGREES*

Goals.   (1) To build arm strength and accuracy in throwing. (2) To develop weight shift from the back leg to the front leg in making long-distance throws.

Skills Emphasized:

- throwing (proper stride and arm path)
- weight shift (gaining momentum)

Procedure.   This is the same drill as the hip drill for the pitchers. Outfielders work with partners about 25 ft apart. The outfielder needs to mark off his stride line and take a comfortable stride toward the target. With the ball and glove at break point, he pulls the ball down and out of the glove, shifts his weight from back leg to front leg, points the front shoulder and elbow at the desired throwing target, and throws, finishing with the correct follow-through.

Coaching Points.   The outfielder should be throwing with the four-seam grip. He should reach for the sky and make a strong overhand throw.

Safety Concerns.   This drill is designed to strengthen and stretch the arm. If an outfielder throws too hard too early he may develop a tired or sore arm.

<table>
<tr><td>DRILL
3</td><td>MOMENTUM</td></tr>
</table>

Goals. (1) To coordinate the body's momentum in moving toward the desired target as the outfielder prepares to throw the ball. (2) To increase arm strength and quickness.

Skills Emphasized:

- continued movement toward the throwing target
- throwing

Procedure. Outfielders work with partners, squared to one another about 25 ft apart. As the drill continues, they gradually increase the throwing distance until they are throwing the length of the gym or working area. With the ball in the glove, the outfielder takes a crow hop to gain momentum. While gaining momentum, he pulls the ball down and out of the glove, strides, points the glove shoulder and elbow toward the target, and makes a strong overhand throw. This continues until the outfielders are at full distance.

Coaching Points. As with the other throwing drills, proper grip and mechanics are essential. As the outfielders spread apart, be certain that their throws travel in a downward path. This forces the thrower to snap the wrist on release, giving the ball more carry.

Variations. With the same set of partners, one outfielder can roll the ball to his partner (as shown below). The fielding partner gathers the ball and makes a strong overhand throw to his partner. Once they have completed five throws each, they spread apart more.

Safety Concerns. The outfielders will be throwing from long distances and must take care not to overthrow their arms. They must gradually stretch to build endurance and arm strength.

DRILL 4

ANGLED GROUND BALLS

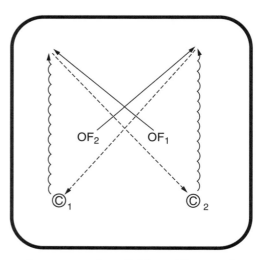

Goals. (1) To develop a proper drop-step angle. (2) To increase pursuit of the ball. (3) To develop fielding and throwing techniques.

Skills Emphasized:

- coordination of footwork
- proper fielding techniques
- increased throwing accuracy

Procedure. You'll need two coaches and a group of outfielders. The coaches stand about 20 to 25 ft apart. Two lines of outfielders are 10 ft in front of and facing the coaches. Coach 1 rolls a ball straight toward the wall. Outfielder 1 opens, chases, and fields the ball. Upon fielding the ball, he turns and throws the ball to Coach 2. Coach 2 rolls the ball straight toward the wall. Outfielder 2 opens, chases, and fields the ball. Upon fielding the ball, he turns and throws the ball to Coach 1. The outfielders continually switch lines, practicing from both angles.

Coaching Points. The outfielder must open with his outside foot angled to where the ball will be fielded. He always should field a moving ball with his glove and make a strong overhand throw to the coach. The coach should vary the speed and the angle of the ball. This will force the outfielder to read the ball and pursue a correct angle.

Variation. This drill can be done with one coach. Using one outfielder at a time, the coach rolls the ball to either side and forces the player to read the angle of the ball.

Safety Concerns. The outfielders will be throwing across the work area. Those not immediately involved in the drill need to be aware of the flight of the ball. Also, the coaches must be aware of all throws. At times, outfielders become lax and throw to the wrong coach. If the walls or work area are not netted, bystanders must be notified that players may make errant throws or that the ball may carom off walls.

DRILL 5

FIELDING ANGLED FLY BALLS

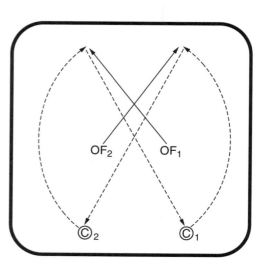

Goals. (1) To develop proper drop-step angles. (2) To increase pursuit in fielding fly balls. (3) To develop fielding techniques. (4) To develop throwing techniques.

Skills Emphasized:

- coordination of footwork
- proper catching techniques
- increased throwing accuracy

Procedure.   Drills for fielding fly balls are designed and run the same way as drills for fielding ground balls. Coach 1 lofts a fly ball. Outfielder 2 opens, chases, and catches the fly ball. After catching the ball, he turns and throws to Coach 2. Coach 2 lofts a fly ball. Outfielder 1 opens, chases, and catches the ball. After catching the ball, he turns and throws to Coach 1. The players rotate lines.

Coaching Points.   In developing a good, quick jump, a proper and even ready position must be mastered. With the outfielder's weight over the balls of his feet and evenly distributed over both legs, he assumes the set position, squared to the plate. This stance allows him to move in any direction at a moment's notice.

On balls hit at an angle, the outfielder should step first with his outside foot at an angle that takes him to the spot that the ball will land. If the ball is hit to his right, he steps first with his right foot. If the ball is hit to his left, he steps first with his left foot.

On balls hit directly over his head, the outfielder should open with the glove-side foot. After making the catch, he stops his momentum over his throwing leg. This shortens the time it takes to get the ball back into the infield. The coaches should loft the balls at different heights and angles to force the outfielder to concentrate on pursuing the proper angle.

Variations.   This drill may use one coach and one group of outfielders. The coach may loft the ball to either side of the fielder, forcing him to read and pursue the ball at all angles.

Safety Concerns.   As with Drill 4, the outfielders will be throwing across the working area. All players and coaches must be alert to all thrown balls.

DRILL

6

FIELDING FLY BALLS DIRECTLY OVERHEAD

Goals.   (1) To develop proper footwork in fielding fly balls. (2) To develop increased arm strength. (3) To develop throwing accuracy.

Skills Emphasized:

- coordination of footwork
- proper catching techniques
- correct throwing mechanics

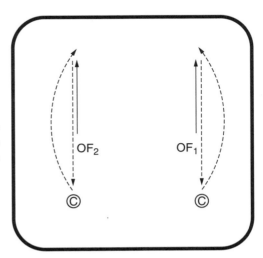

Procedure.   If you're practicing indoors, a normal-size gym is sufficient. Two coaches and two lines of outfielders are needed. The lines of players are about 20 ft apart, with a coach at the head of each line. Each coach tosses a ball over the head of the outfielder. The outfielder opens glove side, chases, and catches the fly ball. After catching the ball, he arrests his momentum on his throwing leg, turns, and throws to the coach at the head of his line. The players continually rotate lines.

Coaching Points.   The outfielder should make a habit of opening with his glove-side foot. The coaches tossing the balls should vary the angles and heights of the tosses to force the outfielders to read them.

Variation.   This drill can be done using one line of outfielders, which will allow coaches and players more room to work angles.

Safety Concerns.   Players not immediately involved in the action must give the fielders room to work. If balls are tossed too far, players are in danger of running into walls.

DRILL 7   *COMMUNICATION*

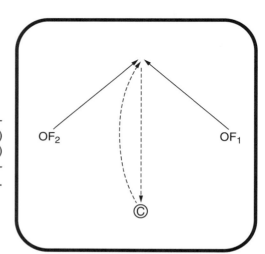

Goals.   (1) To develop communication skills between all outfielders. (2) To develop proper drop angles. (3) To emphasize back-up responsibilities. (4) To develop leadership skills.

Skills Emphasized:

- coordination of footwork
- reading proper angles
- communicating proper calls

Procedure.   If practicing inside, a normal-size gym is sufficient. Two groups of outfielders need to be about 30 ft apart. A coach about 25 ft in front of and between the outfielders tosses the ball in the air. The two outfielders give chase, one making the call and the catch, the other backing up.

Coaching Points.   Communication is essential in this drill. You need to develop a system that allows the outfielders to make calls. We use an *I've got it!* call by the outfielder who will catch the ball. During this drill, make sure everyone can hear the call. This may be embarrassing for the players practicing, but it is not as embarrassing as dropping a fly ball or having two outfielders collide.

Variation.   Using the same set, designate one of the fielders as the center fielder, who leads the drill. Remember that the center fielder has priority calls on all balls. Once he calls *I've got it*, the other outfielders get into position to back him up.

Safety Concerns.   With both fielders giving chase, there is always the chance of a collision. All outfielders must communicate who will catch the ball and who will back up.

PART III
Practice by Skill

We're all familiar with teams that despite outstanding talent can't seem to put it all together into a successful effort. Your ability to fit each player into the overall team effort will determine your team's chances for a successful season.

In Part II we provided drills that stress the skills needed to play each position successfully. We also considered how each position relates to the overall efforts of the team. In Part III, we'll take that one step further and cover the fundamentals of working together as fielders, hitters, and baserunners.

We begin with chapter 8—fielding. Here we share our philosophies and tips on how to prepare your squad to defend all batted balls (grounders, flies, and line-drives), attempted bunts, attempted steals, and emerging rundown situations. Every game situation is different, and it's important that every player knows his role as it relates to the team objectives. To help you provide this information, we've included two drills that stress team unity. These drills help players develop their individual skills for playing their positions, while giving them the opportunity to merge those skills with those of their teammates in game situations.

In chapter 9, we provide 14 drills to help your players become good hitters in different game situations. These drills will aid your players in learning good hitting techniques, developing a quick bat, mastering the strike zone, and becoming good mission hitters. When a player steps to the plate in a game, his mission might be to get on base, move a runner, or drive a runner home. We show you how to provide game situations that allow your hitters to practice and gain enough confidence to meet the missions they face.

Once on base, players can make or break your effort in a split second. Your first step is to analyze your team's ability as baserunners. If your players possess tremendous speed, you'll want to steal more. If your team is slow, you'll want to practice more hit-and-run situations. Whatever the case, your team can be successful on the base path, and we show you how in chapter 10. We offer four drills that stress proper running technique, helping players maximize their ability to quicken acceleration and decrease the time rounding bases. We also include six drills that stress safe sliding skills. These drills work on players' sliding and footwork and their ability to read a pitcher's movements.

Again, the drills in Part III were designed to keep sessions moving and eliminate time wasted by players standing around. We outline the goals of each drill, the skills emphasized, how to perform the drill, and our own coaching tips. We also offer safety tips and variations when appropriate to add diversity to your practice and help you adapt to special circumstances regarding your practice facilities.

CHAPTER 8

Fielding

Each morning, millions of people open their newspapers to the sports section, where the headlines are filled with the names of the players who had game-winning hits or pitched shutout ball. Little attention is given to the player who made the game-saving catch, to the team that played errorless baseball, or to the coach who made a critical defensive move late in the game. Although the importance of defense has always been underrated by the media and fans, coaches know the value of a sound defensive team. It can take only one or two errors to lose a ballgame.

You need to establish a simple, organized system for preparing your team to react to and to master all emerging defensive situations. Communication is essential in teaching and understanding team defense. All players involved must know their correct defensive positioning, cut-offs, relays, and base coverages. The best way to learn team defense is by practicing game situations. To be solid defensively, a team must be able to handle all priority calls, cut-offs, relays, and base coverages based on all situations relative to the

- batted ball,
- attempted bunt,
- attempted steal, and
- emerging rundown situations.

Figure 8.1 lists numerous team defense situations. As you know, the way you will handle each situation—how your team will cover the batted ball, for example—depends on the location of the runners. Your team must know exactly what to do in each situation.

On every pitch, there is the possibility of something happening, so it is critical for all players to understand their role in defensing against every possible situation. Before each pitch is thrown, every defensive player must know what to do once the ball is hit, fielded, and thrown.

If baseball were simple, players would have time to make a decision after they received the ball. But baseball isn't simple. It is a game of reaction—but *practiced* reaction. In developing practiced reactions, it is important that you tell your players what you expect them to do in certain situations. Answering the following questions will help you and your team in each of the following defensive situations.

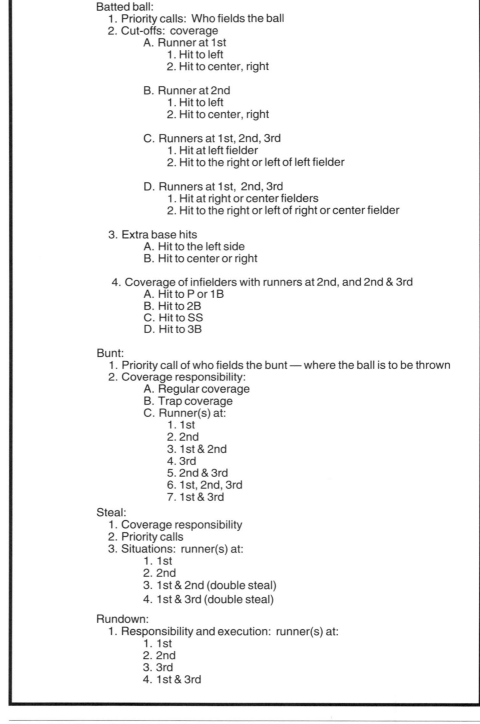

Batted ball:
1. Priority calls: Who fields the ball
2. Cut-offs: coverage
    A. Runner at 1st
        1. Hit to left
        2. Hit to center, right

    B. Runner at 2nd
        1. Hit to left
        2. Hit to center, right

    C. Runners at 1st, 2nd, 3rd
        1. Hit at left fielder
        2. Hit to the right or left of left fielder

    D. Runners at 1st, 2nd, 3rd
        1. Hit at right or center fielders
        2. Hit to the right or left of right or center fielder

3. Extra base hits
    A. Hit to the left side
    B. Hit to center or right

4. Coverage of infielders with runners at 2nd, and 2nd & 3rd
    A. Hit to P or 1B
    B. Hit to 2B
    C. Hit to SS
    D. Hit to 3B

Bunt:
1. Priority call of who fields the bunt — where the ball is to be thrown
2. Coverage responsibility:
    A. Regular coverage
    B. Trap coverage
    C. Runner(s) at:
        1. 1st
        2. 2nd
        3. 1st & 2nd
        4. 3rd
        5. 2nd & 3rd
        6. 1st, 2nd, 3rd
        7. 1st & 3rd

Steal:
1. Coverage responsibility
2. Priority calls
3. Situations: runner(s) at:
    1. 1st
    2. 2nd
    3. 1st & 2nd (double steal)
    4. 1st & 3rd (double steal)

Rundown:
1. Responsibility and execution: runner(s) at:
    1. 1st
    2. 2nd
    3. 3rd
    4. 1st & 3rd

Figure 8.1   Team defense situations.

The Batted Ball

Priority Calls: Who fields the ball?
Communication: Where should the ball be thrown?
Cut-offs: Who handles the throw?
Coverage: Who covers each base?

An Attempted Bunt

Priority Calls: What do you do to hold the runner? Are there any special coverages?
Communication: Who fields the ball? Where do you throw the ball?
Coverage: Is every possible situation covered? Who covers each base?

An Attempted Steal

Priority Calls: What do you do to hold the runner? Are there any special plays?
Communication: How do you know if there is a steal?
Cut-offs: Who handles the throw?
Coverage: How do you handle coverage at the bag? Is every possible situation covered?

Emerging Rundowns

Priority Calls: Do you use the two-man system (in which you do not mind chasing the runner to the next base) or the three-man system (in which you chase the runner back to the original base)?
Communication: Who is responsible for calls?
Cut-offs: Who will be the cut-off man? Who will be the relay man?
Coverage: How do you handle coverages at the bag?

TEAM DEFENSE DRILLS

Once you have developed your overall philosophy of team defense, you can establish a practice time for each group of situations. You can incorporate the drills in the time and space you devote to mastering basic skills. Concentrate on one situation one day (such as a man on first). The next day focus on a man on second. Follow this until you have covered all possible situations.

DRILL
1   *LITTLE LEAGUE*

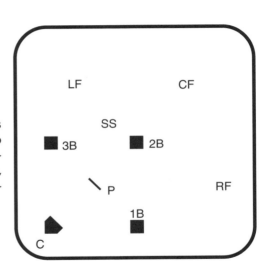

Goals. (1) To establish priority calls for all batted-ball situations. (2) To develop communication skills between all players. (3) To develop, learn, and understand defensive coverages.

Skills Emphasized:

- player communication
- proper movement of players

Procedure.   Construct an infield with the bases about 40 ft apart. Place all eight everyday players and a pitcher at their positions. The set-up should reflect a Little League situation. A coach is needed to stand behind the catcher. Place a runner in your desired situation and put a batter at the plate. Simply throw the ball to an area and make a call as to what kind of hit it is, single, double, or triple. Based on your calls (such as: man on first, no one out, double to the eight-center gap), the players move to their correct positions working on calls, relays, cuts, and base coverages. With the Little League set, you may work on all batted-ball, attempted bunt, attempted steal, and emerging rundown situations.

Coaching Points.   Little League is one of the best drills for helping your players understand the whole defensive scheme. Players must communicate their correct positioning, proper relays, and cuts. As a coach, you control the situations. Make the players understand and cover all possible emerging plays.

Safety Concerns.   Because of the number of players involved in this drill, everyone must be conscientious at all times. The players should move at half-speed and all throws should be soft.

DRILL
2   *FULL INFIELD*

Goals.   (1) To establish priority calls based on all situations involving attempted bunts, attempted steals, and emerging rundowns. (2) To develop communication skills between all players. (3) To develop timing between all players. (4) To develop, learn, and understand defensive coverages.

Skills Emphasized:

- communication
- proper movement of players
- proper alignment of players

Procedure.   If space permits, construct a regular-size infield. Infielders go to their positions and a pitcher goes to the mound. Baserunners need to be available to create situations and to run. One coach is needed to tell the players the situation. For example, the coach may say, *runner on third, one out.* He puts a runner on third and then hits a ground ball to a player. The infielders and pitcher must react as if they are playing a real game. From this set-up, you can work on all situations involving infielders.

Coaching Points.   The players and pitchers likely to see the most action during the season should be involved in the majority of the drills. This drill will allow you to work on all batted-ball, attempted bunt, attempted steal, and emerging rundown situations. If you are unable to fit a full infield into your available space, make your area as big as possible.

Variations.   Some aspects of team defense allow you to concentrate on a specific situation, such as rundowns. Place the pitcher's mound at one end of your practice area. Then, depending on who you want to work with, construct a half-infield. In this case, work with the first baseman and your middle infielders. Now, you can work on rundowns between first and second. The pitcher gets on the mound and comes to the set position. A baserunner is at first, and the fielders are at their positions. The pitcher picks the runner off first base, and a rundown occurs. This can be accomplished using any situation.

Safety Concerns. Because hard balls will be used in these live drills, all baserunners should be wearing helmets. Also, it is important that the runners and infielders know the situations. This will keep them from being in the wrong place at the wrong time.

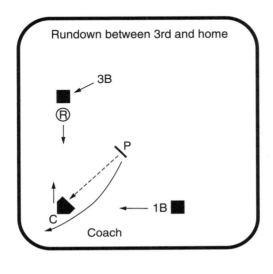

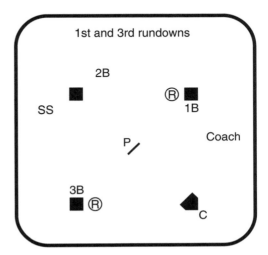

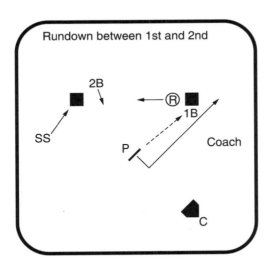

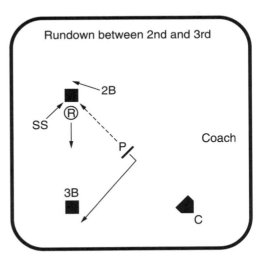

CHAPTER 9

Hitting

Ted Williams, former Boston Red Sox standout and the last major leaguer to hit .400 in a complete season, once said, "To be a good hitter, you must be quick with the bat and get a good pitch to hit." Our philosophy concurs and advises: Look at the ball, develop a level shoulder-to-shoulder swing, rotate the hips, and gain momentum to the pitcher.

When working with hitters, develop a simple routine that enables them to gain quickness with the bat and master the strike zone. The routine should give hitters a chance to improve hand quickness through a number of mandatory repetitions and to work on eliminating any problems that slow the swing. The routine also should provide live hitting opportunities, so your hitters can master the strike zone and develop mission hitting.

In developing hitters, we believe in two types of hitting, batting practice and live hitting. Batting practice develops hitters through 250 swings. This comes through heavy bat, tee drills, toss-and-hit drills, and half cage. Live hitting provides game experience through live pitching. Hitters can be put into situations with counts such as 2-and-1 with a man on first.

In developing good practice drills for team offense, look at the overall team concept and hitting abilities of each player. Know your projected batting order for the coming season. Know the overall strengths and weaknesses of your team. If your team is loaded with great pitchers and has a strong defense but is weak in hitting, you will want to devise a system to develop a way of scraping up runs. If you are fortunate enough to have a great hitting team that produces 8 to 10 runs a game, count your blessings. But you must also still develop a hitting scheme to score those.

PHILOSOPHY

Actions always speak louder than words. It is easy for a coach to say, We are going to score runs by doing this or that. But if a team does not prepare properly, many of those baserunners will not cross the plate. When developing your team offensive philosophy, keep things simple. Players have enough to worry about as the game develops. The easier your philosophy is to understand, the easier it is to execute. A good, clear, and simple rule to follow is mission hitting.

Mission Hitting

Every at-bat provides the hitter with a challenge and a mission. That mission may be to get on base, to move a runner, or to drive in a runner. If no one is on base, the hitter must try and get on. If there is a runner on base, the hitter must find a way of advancing the runner and keep the inning going. If there is a runner in scoring position, the hitter must find a way to drive the runner in, or at least to extend the inning so someone else may drive the runner in.

In practice, provide game situations that allow your hitters to practice and become confident in mission hitting. The situations you develop will need to reflect the different hitting counts and possible experiences a hitter may face.

Developing a Quick Bat

The hitting drills you incorporate should emphasize four key factors, including

- chin (for the look at the ball),
- shoulder (for the shoulder-to-shoulder swing),
- knee (for gained momentum and shift of the weight), and
- heel (for proper hip drive and follow-through).

Players should practice these four factors as they develop the correct swing through a number of mandatory repetitions. The repetitions should include the use of heavy or weighted bats, hitting tees, toss-and-hit drills, half-cage swings, batting practice, and live hitting.

Mastering the Strike Zone

As a hitter, one of the toughest mental flaws to overcome is swinging at balls out of the strike zone or chasing pitches that are hard to drive. As a coach, you need to develop a routine that makes hitting good pitches automatic. One of the easiest ways to master the strike zone is through simulated game situations. These situations may be developed during the time and space allotted for live pitching and hitting.

HEAVY BAT DRILLS

The heavy bat routine is a set of drills designed to strengthen and quicken the wrists while the hitter concentrates on developing good hitting mechanics. There are seven drills, each consisting of 10 repetitions.

DRILL 1 | HIP DRILL

Goals. (1) To develop a proper stance. (2) To develop proper weight shift. (3) To increase use of the hips.

Skills Emphasized:

- stride
- hip rotation
- rotation of back heel
- look at the ball

Procedure. Holding the bat behind his back, the hitter assumes his stance. As the hitter takes his stride toward the pitcher, he shifts his weight from back leg to front knee, rotates his back heel to make use of the hips, and finishes with his back knee pointing toward the front knee. Once in the finished position, the barrel of the bat should be at the point of contact.

Coaching Points. The hitter must develop a proper stride and stay on balance. As he rotates his hips and heel, his chin should finish over his back shoulder. This will force him to get a good look at the ball.

DRILL 2 | AX DRILL I

Goals. (1) To develop and strengthen the wrists. (2) To quicken the hands.

Skills Emphasized:

- proper grip
- extension of the arms

Procedure.   With the bat in both hands and arms extended at chin height, the hitter raises the bat over his head, touches his backside, and brings the bat back to the starting point, as though he is chopping wood.

Coaching Points.   The hitter should have a proper hitting grip. As he lowers the bat in front of his face, it should go no lower than his chin.

DRILL 3   AX DRILL II

Goals.   (1) To develop and strengthen the wrists. (2) To quicken the hands.
Skills Emphasized:

- proper grip

Procedure.   With the bat in both hands and arms extended at chin height, the hitter moves his wrists up and down, taking the bat from the starting point and, moving his wrists only, bringing it to his hitting shoulder and then back to the starting point.
Coaching Point.   As the hitter lowers the bat in front, it should go no lower than his chin.

DRILL 4

SHOULDER, CONTACT, SHOULDER

Goals. (1) To develop a proper swing. (2) To increase bat speed. (3) To develop a proper look at the ball.

Skills Emphasized:

- proper grip
- proper starting point of bat
- proper motion and extension of the arms
- correct follow-through

Procedure. Assuming his stance, the batter's hands should be at the starting point of the swing, the bat even with his back shoulder, his hands even with the armpit and back knee. The hitter gains momentum in the plain of the swing, going from the back shoulder to contact point, arms extended, and finishes the swing, emphasizing the look at the ball, shift of weight to the front knee, rotation of the back heel and hips.

Coaching Points. This drill is not intended to be a race to see who can finish his swings first. The goal is to motion 10 perfect swings. Each hitter, concentrating on the perfect swing, should simulate an at-bat, with a focus on getting a good look at the ball.

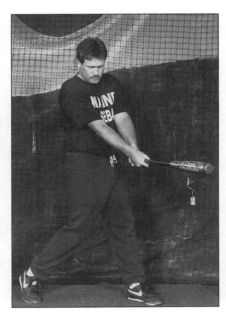

DRILL 5   *SHOULDER-TO-SHOULDER SWING*

Goals.   (1) To achieve momentum in the path of the swing as you take the bat from shoulder to shoulder. (2) To develop and emphasize all aspects of the swing.

Skills Emphasized:

- grip
- proper starting point of bat
- motion and extension of the arms
- follow-through

Procedure.   This drill is similar to Drill 4, but here the hitter doesn't stop at contact point. The hitter should assume his proper stance with the bat at its starting point of the swing. The hitter strides to the simulated pitch and practices a full swing, ending with the bat against his front shoulder.

Coaching Points.   Again, this is not a race. The goal is to master the perfect swing and concentrate on getting a good look at the ball.

DRILL

6   *TOP-HAND DRILL*

Goals.   (1) To develop top-hand strength. (2) To increase bat speed.

Skills Emphasized:

- top-hand grip
- swing
- follow-through

Procedure.   This drill is performed the same way as the shoulder-to-shoulder drill, except you only use the top hand. This drill develops coordination of the top hand in rotation with the hips and back heel.

Coaching Point.   The hitter should choke up on the bat. This will allow him to stay on balance and keep control of the bat as he attempts the perfect swing.

DRILL 7   HIT-AND-RUN

Goals.   (1) To develop skills for hitting the ball to the opposite field. (2) To develop weight shift.

Skills Emphasized:

- increased weight-shift timing
- look at the ball
- follow-through

Procedure.   The hitter should take his stride while keeping his hands back at the starting point, even with the back knee, and with the front shoulder in. He should visualize the look at the ball, swing, and belly-button the ball to the opposite field, finishing with the appropriate follow-through.

Coaching Points.   The goal is to keep the weight and hands back while striding toward the pitch. As the hitter begins to transfer his weight, he must keep his head and shoulder in and drive the ball to the opposite field. When the swing is completed, the hitter's belly-button should be pointing toward the path of the ball.

HITTING DRILLS

The most efficient way to develop hitters and provide game situations is to incorporate both live hitting and live pitching. The goal of live hitting is to slowly develop the proper hitting mechanics while allowing the hitters time to adjust to the increased speeds and different rotations of each pitch. By facing live pitching, the hitter learns to adjust to the strike zone while seeing the ball leave the pitcher's hand. This allows the hitters and pitchers to progress at the same pace, which saves time. Our goal with the five hitting drills that follow is to get quick with the bat. We want our players to be able to generate the highest possible bat speed in the shortest amount of time. The following drills allow this and afford the hitter the opportunity to check his swing and to get maximum repetitions.

DRILL
8   *TEE DRILLS*

Goals.   (1) To develop and ensure that the hitter makes contact with the barrel of the bat. (2) To develop the hitter's focus on looking at the ball with the chin finishing over the back shoulder. (3) To develop a swing that allows the hitter to hit the ball to all parts of the field.

Skills Emphasized:

- look at the ball
- proper swing

Procedure.   Using tees is often efficient because you need only one person to practice. Using the tee allows the hitter to place the ball where he wants it, on the inside, down the middle, or on the outside part of the plate. It allows him to work on the different areas to which the ball can be pitched.

Coaching Points.   The hitter should use a regular bat. He should place the tee at different areas within the strike zone to simulate the location of different pitches.

DRILL 9   SOFT TOSS

Goals.   (1) To develop and master the strike zone, increase bat speed, develop a proper swing, and master mission hitting. (2) To get a maximum number of repetitions.

Skills Emphasized:

- look at the ball
- swing
- concentration

Procedure.   You need two people: a hitter and a tosser. You also need a netted or soft area to hit the ball into. The hitter assumes hitting position. The tosser is positioned about 10 ft from the hitter at a 45-degree angle away from the direction of the swing.

The mission of soft toss is the same as the tee drill—to ensure that the hitter is getting the right look at the ball and that he is making contact at the fat of the bat. Young, undisciplined hitters tend to pull the head to watch the flight of the ball. The emphasis is on the four key factors of hitting: chin, shoulder, knee, and heel. The difference here is that the hitter must concentrate on seeing a moving ball.

The tosser flips the ball underhanded into the hitting zone. The hitter, focusing on a proper swing, drives the ball into the netted area. This drill allows the hitter and tosser to focus on the correct swing. It also allows for many repetitions in a short amount of time.

Coaching Points.   It is critical for the tosser to be at a 45-degree angle from the hitter. The tosser should toss the ball to an area within the hitting zone. This will force the hitter to drive the ball into the netted area and away from the tosser.

DRILL
10 | *SHORT TOSS OR HALF CAGE*

Goals. (1) To develop a proper swing, increase bat speed, learn the strike zone, and develop mission hitting. (2) To get a maximum number of repetitions.

Skills Emphasized:

- proper look and swing at live pitching
- increased awareness of the hitter's power zone

Procedure. You will need two people, a batting cage, an L-screen, and baseballs. The hitter takes his hitting position with the pitcher or tosser about 30 ft away and behind the L-screen. The tosser throws the ball to different locations within the strike zone. The hitter makes contact straight away. Attempting to drive the ball back at the screen allows the hitter the most concentrated look at the ball while gaining extension with the arms.

Coaching Points. The ball should be thrown into different locations within the strike zone. This will force the batter to hit the ball where it is pitched. The tosser can also spin the ball to simulate the movement of a breaking ball.

Safety Concerns. The hitter should always have a helmet. The tosser must be aware that batted balls will be hit back up the middle. The tosser, after releasing the ball, must be behind the L-screen for maximum protection.

DRILL 11   FULL CAGE, LIVE HITTING

Goals.   (1) To master the strike zone. (2) To develop the proper swing and mission hitting.

Skills Emphasized:

- swing

- concentration

Procedure.   This drill puts Drills 1 through 10 together. It is the same as the half-cage drill but this drill is from 60 ft, 6 in. Either have your tosser throw as if he is throwing batting practice, or simulate game situations by using live pitching.

Coaching Points.   This is a great time to develop both hitters and pitchers. If you have a full hitting cage or two, simulate game situations. Hitters get to see live pitchers and vice versa.

Safety Concerns.   In this drill, balls will be flying all over the place. Hitters should wear helmets. Use an L-screen to protect the pitcher from batted balls. Do not attempt this drill outside of a batting cage or netted area.

DRILL 12 LIVE HITTING

Goals. (1) To develop hitting abilities. (2) To master the strike zone. (3) To become used to seeing live pitching.

Skills Emphasized:

- look at the ball
- concentrated hitting

Procedure. This drill allows for simultaneous development of hitters and pitchers. For maximum protection, do this drill in a batting cage or cages. The cage area should be well lighted, with a pitcher's mound in its appropriate spot (60 ft, 6 in. from home plate) and an L-screen in front of the mound to protect the pitcher.

All pitchers who need to throw for the day can get their work in playing against live hitters. If one cage is available, two pitchers may be developed at the same time. With two cages, four pitchers may be developed at once. The pitchers will alternate innings as under game conditions.

Establish a group of hitters to hit each half-inning. If you use regular at-bat conditions beginning with a two-ball, one-strike count, three hitters can get the sufficient number of at-bats. If it is a hit-and-run or run-and-hit situation, four to five hitters may effectively be involved.

Once the pitchers are ready, start game situations. The count is 2 and 1. The pitcher works on throwing the ball to location. The hitter tries to make contact and drive the ball to the point from where it is pitched. Once the pitcher has finished the required number of pitches, bring in another pitcher and a new group of hitters.

Coaching Points. Your starters need to get the maximum number of repetitions to prepare them for the season. The pitchers should follow their regular pitching routine for the season. If they need to throw three innings of 15 pitches, two pitchers will have to alternate innings until both are completed. Then you can bring in more pitchers.

Variations. If you're practicing indoors and your facility is large enough and offers maximum protection, you can play indoor games. If there's not enough room for a game, try for a full infield, excluding outfielders from defensive play. Place a portable mound in the middle of the facility with an L-screen in front of the mound.

Safety Concerns. If you are indoors, be sure the area is well lighted. Cover all areas with protection, as discussed in chapter 2. The players must know that balls coming off the floor move much more quickly than balls coming off turf.

BUNTING DRILLS

As with any aspect of the game of baseball, you need to develop a philosophy in relation to the bunting game. This philosophy should be developed around your team's strengths and weaknesses. If you have a strong pitching staff and little hitting, you may need to bunt more to score runs. If your players are slow, power hitters, bunting may not be a priority.

The bunt can be an explosive weapon for many teams. The element of surprise caused by the squeeze bunt or the base-hit bunt will often pressure the opposition into making mental mistakes. The ability to move runners along via the sacrifice bunt can mean the difference between winning and losing a game.

As you organize practice sessions involving the bunt, develop your team to be adept in bunting, especially if the bunt will be a team weapon. All players, from power-hitting outfielders to scrappy-hitting second basemen, must be able to lay the sacrifice bunt down both baselines. Players with better-than-average speed should use the base-hit bunt as a tool for getting on base.

DRILL
13 | *TWO-LINE BUNTING*

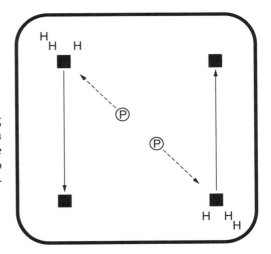

Goals. (1) To develop bunting skills. (2) To increase quickness in getting out of the box. (3) To increase player confidence in bunting. (4) To develop proper bat angles and maximize repetitive opportunities.

Skills Emphasized:

- hand- and footwork
- concentration
- knowledge of bunting situations
- mastering the strike zone

Procedure.   Place four bases in diamond formation about 60 ft apart. Place two throwers in the middle, throwing in the opposite direction. Hitters take turns bunting and getting out of the box. Hitters rotate lines.

Coaching Points.   Tell the hitter what type of bunt to practice and where to bunt the ball. Make sure hitters bunt strikes only. After the ball is bunted, hitters should practice getting out of the box, using proper running form.

Variation—Four-line bunting.   To increase the number of repetitions for each hitter, place four throwers in the center and have hitters at each corner. This can be used as a conditioning drill.

Safety Concerns.   Hitters must be aware of foul balls, rolling balls, and dropped bats.

LIVE BUNTING

Goals.   (1) To increase bunting skills. (2) To develop bat angles. (3) To be involved in game situations.

Skills Emphasized:

- hand- and footwork
- concentration
- knowledge of bunting situations
- mastering the strike zone

Procedure.   You'll need batting cages, a hitter, a catcher, and a pitcher. The three players take their positions, with the hitter and pitcher 60 ft, 6 in. apart. The pitcher works from the stretch. The hitter assumes his hitting stance. You give the situation (such as squeeze) and the hitter bunts the ball to the appropriate place.

Coaching Points.   If the situation calls for a sacrifice bunt, the hitter must bunt the ball before attempting to get out of the box. To simulate getting out of the box, have the bunter attempt the first two steps toward first. If the hitter is attempting to bunt for a hit, he must not give his decision away too early.

Safety Concerns.   Due to possible foul balls, the netted area should be fully enclosed and well lighted. The hitter must wear a helmet and the catcher be fully geared.

CHAPTER 10

Baserunning

Speed kills, or so the adage goes. Every great baseball team has a few athletes with great speed. Those who lack great speed make up for it with proper form, aggressive approaches, and knowledge of the game.

No matter how poor of a hitting day your players may be having, if they know how to run the bases, there is always that chance of stealing a run or two.

Coach's Corner

I believe the game is won with the bat. More often than not, I am going to let my players swing the bat to win the game. I also understand we may be facing a great pitcher that day, one who can throw the ball to location, mix speeds, and get my hitters out. If this is the case, I must try to generate some offense another way. If my players know how to run, we can often score a run without the use of a hit.

Players with below-average speed can still be great baserunners. They can make up for their lack of speed by getting good jumps, reading and anticipating the situation, understanding the game, and being aggressive.

PHILOSOPHY

Each coach has his own philosophy on baserunning. Your philosophy may differ from year to year depending on your team's ability. If you have a great baserunning team, you may use the steal more. If they are poor baserunners, you may have them involved in more hit-and-runs. To maximize your team's ability to run, teach each player to run in a way that maximizes acceleration, practice game situations, and use outs appropriately.

Our philosophy is to develop two leads that will aid our baserunners. The first is a safe lead used to get a secondary lead for a delayed steal or a hit-and-run. The second is a steal lead used for a straight steal or a run-and-hit.

At Maine, we let the players swing away. If we want to run, we will more often than not protect the runner with the hit-and-run. By utilizing the hit-and-run, we protect the runner more by moving the fielders and letting the hitter put the ball into play.

PRACTICE APPROACH

Baserunning can be practiced anywhere—from the gym, to a hallway, to a classroom. Many practice activities offer opportunities to work on baserunning: practice game situations, such as the steal, the hit-and-run, the run-and-hit; and any form of movement using the bat, such as the bunt and getting out of the batter's box.

Be sure to practice all the aspects of baserunning and do so as if you were in a game. If you are working on moving runners with the bat, your hitter and runners must be synchronized. Each time, in game situations, tell the hitter and runner the situation, steal or hit-and-run; and what they should be attempting to do in each situation. Address proper running form, sliding, and safety. Once their baserunning fundamentals are solid, your runners will develop the confidence necessary to round the bases aggressively and wisely.

BASERUNNING DRILLS

Some people are blessed with blinding speed. Others are not so fortunate. But there is hope for those who seem to have lead in their shoes. While proper running technique may not make your players world-class sprinters, it will help maximize their ability to quicken acceleration and decrease the time rounding the bases. The following drills will help you stress proper running technique.

DRILL 1 *FORM RUNNING*

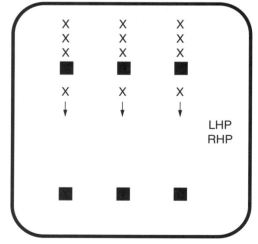

Goals. (1) To increase running efficiency. (2) To decrease running distance.

Skill Emphasized:

- proper body movements and angles

Procedure. Form three even lines of runners. Each line should be about 10 ft apart. Mark a straight line for players to run on. If possible, this line should be 90 ft long. In slow motion, the players walk up the line using the correct running form. Once all have completed the distance, they turn around and do it again. As they increase repetitions, they can begin to move quicker until they are running at full speed.

Coaching Points.   The goal of this drill is to develop proper running form while decreasing the actual number of steps taken, so it is important to begin slow, while concentrating on the correct actions. As the runners get better, you can increase the speed. Use these tips when coaching form running:

- Eyes should be focused on the running target (the line).
- Head should be up and body and hands loose.
- Arms should pump in piston fashion, up and down with elbows at sides.
- Run on the balls of the feet, with toes pointing to the target, knees bent, and legs lifted high.

We are not track coaches and do not pretend to be. To increase our knowledge and teaching skills, we have consulted track coaches, strength coaches, and doctors to learn more about running form. We would advise all baseball coaches to do the same.

DRILL 2 — STEAL-AND-HIT

Goals.   (1) To increase base-running skills and simulate stealing situations. (2) To increase efficiency in getting out of the box.

Skills Emphasized:

- proper steal reads
- proper leads
- proper footwork

Procedure: *Steal.* Form three even lines of runners 10 ft apart. If possible, the lines should be 90 ft long. Place a portable base at the end of each line, six bases in all. The first runners of each line assume a steal lead. Place a pitcher at an appropriate spot to simulate game situations. The pitcher attempts to simulate a throw over to first or deliver the ball home. The runners make a read and take the necessary steps in regards to the situation. The runners sprint down the line to the base and then waits for the rest to finish.

Procedure: *Hit.* Turn the lines around to face the opposite direction. Each line will need a bat. The base will be home plate. The pitcher needs to be on the other side of the facility, opposite the steal pitcher. This pitcher simulates delivering a pitch to the plate. The first hitter of each line simulates a swing, drops the bat, and gets out of the box. This will continue until each hitter has had a turn.

Coaching Points.   Simulate game situations. Tell each runner if he has a safe lead, a steal lead, a hit-and-run lead, a run-and-hit lead, or a bunt lead. This will force him to concentrate on the situation and focus on the game. The hitters need to practice getting out of the box and running in a straight line. The pitcher should only simulate throwing the ball. You can use both left- and right-handed pitchers to give the runners and hitters different reads. Run this drill as long as you deem necessary.

DRILL 3

SINGLE-LINE BASERUNNING

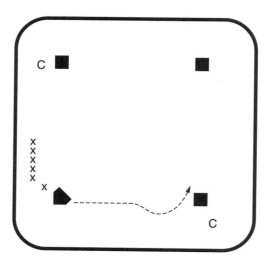

Goals.   (1) To increase baserunning skills. (2) To increase efficiency in getting out of the box. (3) To increase cardiovascular strength.

Skills Emphasized:

- footwork

- proper running angles

Procedure.   If possible, construct a diamond with the bases 90 ft apart. Line the hitters up at home plate. Put a pitcher on the mound and coaches at each base. The pitcher simulates delivering the ball to the plate. One at a time, each hitter swings and runs the designated hit—single, double, triple, or inside-the-park home run.

Coaching Points.   Designate a lead runner. Each time that runner returns to the head of the line, change the type of hit. This is a great communication drill between the base coaches and the runners. Make sure the baserunners read the signs of the coaches and become accustomed to understanding the signals.

Safety Concerns.   If you have to use portable bases, make sure they are stationary. If they slip, use tape instead to mark the location of the bases.

DRILL
4 | FOUR BASES

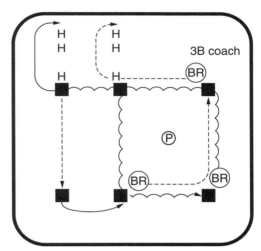

Goals.   (1) To increase baserunning skills at every base and the plate. (2) To increase cardiovascular fitness.
Skills Emphasized:

- angles

- footwork

- reads

Procedure.   Construct the same diamond as in Drill 3. Add an extra home plate and first base alongside the regular two. They should be about 10 ft apart. Place a runner at each of the original three bases. Split the rest of the runners into two groups and place them in single-file lines at the two home plates. Place a pitcher on the mound.

The pitcher works from the stretch. The baserunners take their leads. The first two hitters each have a bat and take their stance at home plate. The pitcher comes to the set position and simulates a delivery to the plate.

The baserunners run to their designated destinations. The hitter closest to the plate takes a full swing and runs out a double. The hitter furthest from the pitcher bunts for a hit-and-run to the outside of first base. Once at first, he moves to the inside first base and takes his lead. The runner who was originally at first runs to third. The original runner at second scores, running to the furthest plate and going to the end of that line. The original runner at third scores at the first plate and goes to the end of that line. Once this has been completed, all bases should be full of runners and the next two hitters step to the plate.

Again, the pitcher comes to the set and simulates pitch delivery, and the drill continues. If the runners go to the correct bases, they will continually rotate and get repetitions at each base.

Coaching Points.   This is a fantastic baserunning drill. It covers most baserunning situations and involves five players with each pitch.

Safety Concerns.   This drill is confusing. It would be advisable to walk through the running stations with your players the first few times. Because of the number of players involved, never use a thrown or live ball. Hitters must be aware of swinging bats.

SLIDING DRILLS

One aspect of teaching baseball that is frequently overlooked is sliding. Yet, sliding is the most dangerous area in the game. Incorrect sliding technique can lead to sprained ankles, twisted knees, broken fingers, and swollen faces.

Practice sliding at least four times a week. It develops three areas important in building a good team: safety, confidence, and desire.

Safety should be the main focus when conducting practice. A healthy team makes for a better team. If you've ever had your best players out with injuries, you know this is true. By properly developing sliding skills, you reduce the risk of injury and increase the chance of scoring more runs.

Players who know how to slide are more aggressive and confident in their baserunning skills. A player who slides well will have less hesitation in trying to move to the next base. He knows that on close plays his sliding abilities mean the difference between being safe or out.

All good, hard-nosed players like to get dirty. They like the feeling of making a difference in the outcome of the game. When you teach sliding skills, you are teaching that desire that will make the difference in the outcome of the game.

DRILL

5

SLIDING PUSH DRILL

Goals. (1) To develop proper sliding skills in a controlled setting. (2) To involve all players in a limited amount of time and space. (3) To instill an aggressive style of confidence and play.

Skills Emphasized:

- sliding

- footwork

- reading movement

Procedure. All players should be wearing long pants. We recommend wearing no shoes. Spread the players evenly across the gym and have each sit on the right side of his rear-end with his right leg bent at 90 degrees and curled under his left leg, which is extended yet relaxed. This is the position for the bent-leg slide. The players push themselves across the gym floor using their hands.

Once they have reached one end of the gym, have them turn over, get into

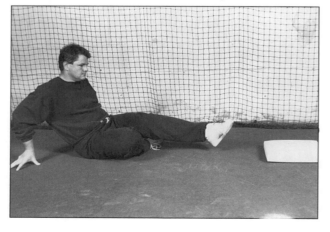

bent-leg slide position with the left leg, and push themselves back across the gym. After enough repetitions, players will be able to use the bent-leg slide from either direction.

Coaching Point. This drill may seem foolish to the players, but they need to understand the importance of proper sliding technique. Explain this to them before starting the drill.

Safety Concerns. Check the sliding area before beginning this drill. Look for objects that may stick into the body or that are loose and could pop up and injure the player. Don't allow the players to sit on their curled leg. Sliding on top of the curled leg can cause injury.

DRILL 6   TWO-STEP SLIDE

Goal.   To develop proper sliding techniques in a controlled setting.

Skills Emphasized:

- sliding
- footwork
- reading movement

Procedure.   This drill is similar to the Sliding Push Drill. Again players should be in long pants (we recommend no shoes), and spread out evenly across the gym. Using the skills from the Sliding Push Drill, the players take two steps and slide, using the bent-leg slide. Once they have gone the length of the gym, they reverse direction, switch, and return to the other end using the same technique and alternating the bent-leg slides on both the left- and right-hand side.

Coaching Points.   The players need to gain enough momentum to slide properly. They must take two good, hard steps before sliding. If not, they will tend to sit, instead of slide.

Safety Concerns.   If your facilities do not provide a safe and effective sliding area, you can purchase sliding mats from any sporting goods store—or you can make your own.

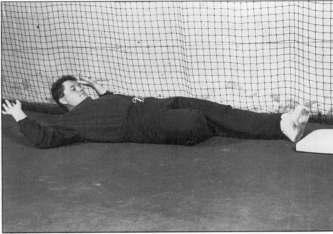

DRILL 7 | *STEAL SLIDE*

Goals.   (1) To develop a good lead and learn to develop a good jump. (2) To develop proper footwork and learn proper sliding technique.

Skills Emphasized:

- proper steal footwork
- proper running form
- proper sliding technique

Procedure.   Players should have long pants on (we recommend wearing no shoes). Organize your players into three even lines. The first group takes a steal lead. After taking the lead, they take three steps and slide. They get up and go again, continuing until they have reached the end of the facility.

DRILL 8   *POP-UP SLIDE*

Goals.   (1) To develop proper sliding techniques. (2) To distinguish and read fielder reactions. (3) To develop reaction time and footwork for advancement to the next base.

Skills Emphasized:

- footwork
- sliding
- reaction time

Procedure.   Form three even lines and place three bases approximately 20 ft from each line. The first group of players take a lead. On a signal from the coach, they run at half-speed toward the base. As they slide, they pop up and get ready to move to the next base. Once they have completed one slide, they return to the end of the line and the next group goes.

Coaching Points.   Each runner should practice the bent-leg slide and popping up from both the left and right sides. If the player slides with his left foot

extended, he pops up, crosses over with his right foot, and continues to the next base. If he slides with his right foot extended, he pops up, and steps to the next base with his left foot.

As the runner approaches the base, he should focus on reading the imaginary fielder, who would be standing either to the inside or outside of the base. This will force the runner to practice sliding one way or the other. Once runners master the slide, you may insert an infielder into the drill. Now the runner must react to the fielder and which side of the bag he is on, making the slide instinctual.

Safety Concerns.   As with all drills, check the area for any possible dangers. Long pants should be worn to prevent skin burns.

DRILL 9

SLIDE BY BASE

Goal.   To develop footwork and sliding technique.

Skills Emphasized:

- footwork
- sliding

Procedure.   Organize three even lines. Place a set of bases about 20 ft from each line. Place another set of bases 20 ft further down.

The first set of players takes a lead. On a signal, they run at half-speed to the base. On the first attempt, they slide by and to the right of the base. As they pass by, they roll to their left, reach back, and tag the base with their right hand.

The first group gets up and takes another lead. They will be heading to the second set of bases. The next group takes a lead. On a coach's signal, both groups run at half-speed to the bases.

The group that has already gone slides to the left and by the base. As they slide by, they turn, reach back, and tag the base with their left hand. Meanwhile, Group 2 does what Group 1 did on its first slide.

Coaching Point.   As the players slide by the bag, they should begin to roll as their shoulder comes even with the bag. Rotate sliding on both sides of the bag and get players used to using both hands.

Safety Concerns.   As the players slide, it is important to slide with their faces away from the bag. This will keep them from getting hit by the ball. Also, check the sliding area for any materials that may cause injury. Players should have on long pants to prevent sliding burns.

DRILL 10 | *HEAD-FIRST SLIDE*

Goals.   (1) To decrease chances of injury. (2) To develop footwork and sliding techniques.

Skills Emphasized:

- footwork
- sliding and reaching techniques
- reading of fielders' actions

Procedure.   Organize three even lines. Place a set of bases about 20 ft from the lines. The first group of players take a lead. As you give the signal, the players run at half-speed to the base. When they are about 8 ft from the base, they slide head first into the base, reaching for it with their hands. After they complete one slide, they return to the end of the line until it is their turn to go again.

Coaching Points.   As the players begin to slide into the base, they should push off with one leg and lunge to the base with the arms and fingers extended to the base. Even though the arms and fingers are extended, they should be relaxed and slightly bent to avoid jamming. Most of the sliding and weight distribution will take place on the chest and stomach.

Safety Concerns.   Although it is an effective tool, we do not advocate the head-first slide, especially into home plate. We cannot control the natural instinct of what a player does on the field, so we try and teach these instincts to be as safe as possible. It is important for the player to have the arms and fingers relaxed and bent to prevent jamming. The stiffer the arms and fingers, the greater the chance for injury. Players should be fully clothed to prevent sliding burns.

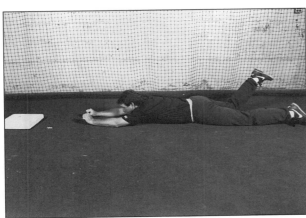

Index

About the Authors

John Winkin racked up more than 900 wins over 40+ years as a coach. During his 22-year tenure as head baseball coach for the University of Maine, he led his team to six College World Series and saw more than 50 of his players drafted into the professional ranks. John is a past president of the American Baseball Coaches Association and has been elected to the Baseball Coaches Hall of Fame and the Maine Baseball Hall of Fame. He has also received the Lefty Gomez Award and ABCA Coach of the Year honors.

In addition to managing, John is a sought-after speaker who presents at clinics nationwide on organizing baseball practice and training indoors.

In his leisure time, John enjoys keeping fit, following sports, and listening to '40s and '50s swing music. He and his wife, Madeline, liver in Orono, Maine.

Jay Kemble is assistant baseball coach and lecturer in physical education at the University of Maine, where his responsibilities include working with the pitching staff and recruiting. He has also coached for the American Legion and Cornell University. Jay pitched under John Winkin for the University of Maine's 1986 College World Series team. He and his wife, Karen, live in Milford, Maine.

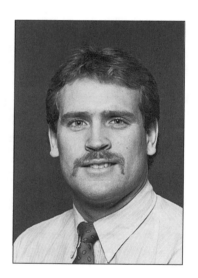

Michael Coutts is the associate head baseball coach at the University of Maine. In addition to his duties as the team's third base coach, Michael instructs players in infield, outfield, and hitting fundamentals. As a collegian, Michael played for John Winkin and captained the 1981 Maine team to the College World Series. He and his wife, Lynn, live in Bangor, Maine.

Additional Baseball Resources

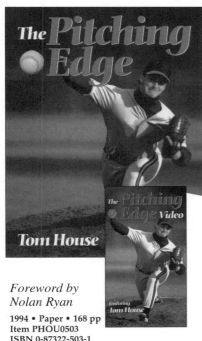

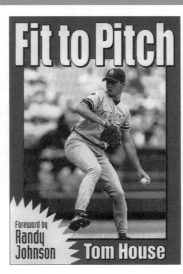

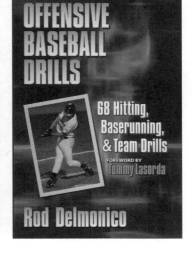

Foreword by Nolan Ryan

1994 • Paper • 168 pp
Item PHOU0503
ISBN 0-87322-503-1
$17.95 ($25.95 Canadian)

(54-minute videotape)

1994 • 1/2" VHS
Item MHOU0414 • ISBN 0-87322-787-5
$29.95 (44.95 Canadian)

Special Book and Video Package
1/2" VHS and *The Pitching Edge* book
Item MHOU0420 • ISBN 0-87322-807-3
$44.95 ($67.50 Canadian)

The Pitching Edge is a practical guide full of cutting-edge information for pitchers and coaches at every level.

The book covers groundbreaking research in pitching mechanics, the latest methods for conditioning the pitcher's total body and throwing arm, and the mental aspects of pitching. The video combines practical on-field instruction and drills with expert off-field analysis and explanation.

Foreword by Randy Johnson, 1995 American League Cy Young Award Winner

1996 • Paper • 216 pp
Item PHOU0882
ISBN 0-87322-882-0
$17.95 ($25.95 Canadian)

Tom House combines his on-field experiences, training with weight room workouts, and years of research to bring you proven, practical applications that will strengthen your pitching throughtout the year. He outlines essential training components to develop more speed, strength, and stamina on the mound; details pitcher-specific workouts for year-round conditioning; and highlights rehabilitation guidelines that help players return to competition faster, safely.

Foreword by Tommy Lasorda

1996 • Paper • 184 pp
Item PDEL0865
ISBN 0-87322-865-0
$14.95 ($20.95 Canadian)

Let Rod Delmonico, *Baseball America*'s 1995 National Division I College Coach of the Year, show you 68 of the offensive drills he uses to take his teams to the top.

Offensive Baseball Drills includes 35 hitting drills, 20 baserunning drills, and 13 team drills for coaches to use in practice or for athletes to do at home. Coach Delmonico also explains the purpose of each drill, equipment needs, proper procedures, coaching points, and how to tailor the drills to older and younger athletes.

Prices subject to change.

Human Kinetics
The Premier Publisher for Sports & Fitness
http://www.humankinetics.com/

Place your order using the appropriate telephone number/
address found in the front of this book, or call
TOLL-FREE in the U.S. 1 800 747-4457.